HERE LIES AMERICA

HERE LIES AMERICA

A Collection of Notable Graves

Nancy Eills
and Parker Hayden

HAWTHORN BOOKS, INC.
Publishers-New York
A Howard & Wyndham Company

*For Andrew, Amity, Stephen, Peter,
Philip, and David, with affection*

HERE LIES AMERICA

Copyright © 1978 by Nancy Brewer Eills and E. Parker Hayden, Jr. Copyright under International and Pan-American Copyright Conventions. All rights reserved, including the right to reproduce this book or portions thereof in any form, except for the inclusion of brief quotations in a review. All inquiries should be addressed to Hawthorn Books, Inc., 260 Madison Avenue, New York, New York 10016. This book was manufactured in the United States of America and published simultaneously in Canada by Prentice-Hall of Canada, Limited, 1870 Birchmount Road, Scarborough, Ontario.

Library of Congress Catalog Card Number: 77-072815

ISBN: 0-8015-3425-9

2 3 4 5 6 7 8 9 10

Contents

Acknowledgments ... ix
Introduction ... xi

Writers of the American Experience
Herman Melville ... 2
Eugene Gladstone O'Neill ... 4
Thomas Clayton Wolfe ... 6
Margaret Mitchell Marsh ... 9
John Henry O'Hara ... 10
John Louis Kerouac ... 12

Children's Writers
Louisa May Alcott ... 17
Horatio Alger, Jr. ... 18

Poets
James Russell Lowell ... 22
Walter (Walt) Whitman ... 24
Emily Elizabeth Dickinson ... 27
Robert Lee Frost ... 28

They Live Through a Line or Two
James Lawrence ... 33
Sarah Josepha Buell Hale ... 34
Horace Greeley ... 36
John A. Joyce ... 38

Where Would We Be Without . . .
Samuel Finley Breese Morse ... 42
Walter Hunt ... 45
Henry (Harry) Wright ... 46
Anna M. Jarvis ... 49

Their Names Are Everyday Words
Lydia Estes Pinkham ... 52

William Wallace Smith and Andrew Smith	54
Frank Winfield Woolworth	56
Milton Snavely Hershey	58

You Can't Say One Without the Other
Meriwether Lewis and William Clark	62
Henry Wells and William George Fargo	64
Chang and Eng Bunker	66
Nathaniel Currier and James Merritt Ives	68
Charles Edward Merrill, Edmund Calvert Lynch, Edward Allen Pierce, Charles Erasmus Fenner, II, and Alpheus Crosby Beane	70

Saints and Sinners
Lola Montez	76
James Butler (Wild Bill) Hickok and Martha Jane Cannary (Calamity Jane) Burke	78
William Barclay (Bat) Masterson	80
Lizzie Andrew Borden	82

Winners
James Fisk, Jr.	86
Henrietta Howland Robinson (Hetty) Green	89
John Pierpont Morgan	90
James Buchanan (Diamond Jim) Brady	92

Losers
George Washington Whistler	97
John Augustus Sutter	98
Calvin Nathaniel Payne	100

Agitators and Reformers
Henry David Thoreau	104
Carry Amelia Moore Nation	107
Henry Louis Mencken	108
Martin Luther King, Jr.	110

Naturalists
John Chapman (Johnny Appleseed)	114
Luther Burbank	117
George Washington Carver	118

Molders of the Land
Pierre Charles L'Enfant   122
John Muir   124

Performers
Edwin Thomas Booth   128
Harry Houdini   130
George Michael Cohan   132
Bessie Smith   135
George Herman (Babe) Ruth   136
Tallulah Brockman Bankhead   139
Judy Garland   140
James Byron Dean   142

Legends
Barbara Hauer Fritchie   146
Ichabod B. Crane   148
John Brown   150
John Luther (Casey) Jones   152

Stylemakers
Florenz Ziegfeld, Jr.   157
Vernon Castle Blyth and Irene Foote Castle   158

Artists
Mathew B. Brady   162
Augustus Saint-Gaudens   165
Edward Hopper   166

Tunesmiths
John Philip Sousa   170
Sergei Vasilyevich Rachmaninoff   172
Charles Edward Ives   174
Cole Albert Porter   177
George Gershwin   178

Acknowledgments

All photographs are by the authors, with the exception of the following:

Cover photograph by Clem Fiori.

John Louis Kerouac: Photograph by John Christie, from the *Gloucester Daily Times*. Reprinted by permission of the photographer.

James Lawrence: Photograph by John Eills.

Meriwether Lewis: Photograph courtesy of Tennessee State Library and Archives.

Charles Edward Merrill: Photograph by Vincent J. Miranda.

Charles Erasmus Fenner, II: Photograph by Convention Photography of New Orleans.

James Butler (Wild Bill) Hickok and Martha Jane Cannary (Calamity Jane) Burke: Photograph by Lambert Florin, from his *Tales the Western Tombstones Tell*. Copyright © 1967 by Superior Publishing Co. Reprinted by permission of the publisher.

Carry Amelia Moore Nation: Photograph by Sammie Feeback, courtesy of the *Belton Star-Herald* and Belton Chamber of Commerce, Inc.

Luther Burbank: Photograph by Lambert Florin, from his *Tales the Western Tombstones Tell*. Copyright © 1967 by Superior Publishing Co. Reprinted by permission of the publisher.

John Muir: Photograph by Bev and Dick West.

James Byron Dean: Photograph by Honor Moore, from *James Dean* by Venable Herndon. Reprinted by permission of the photographer.

John Luther (Casey) Jones: Photograph by Charles Clegg, courtesy of the photographer.

Introduction

Here *Lies America* is a collection of photographs of the gravestones of people who have, in one way or another, contributed to the fabric of American life. They are grouped according to the guise in which we remember them today. Each photograph is accompanied by a short sketch, focusing on the play between the immortality each person has achieved and the certain mortality that death and the grave represent.

Why a book about graves? And why these particular people, or corpses?

A grave cult exists. In Deerfield, Massachusetts, tourists relive the past among the old stones that relate tales of death at the hands of the Indians. In Wilkeson, Washington, visitors count the number of children who died during the great influenza epidemic. In Princeton, New Jersey, the inquisitive seek out the grave of Aaron Burr. History is recorded on stones throughout the country.

Each summer, hundreds, who have only an idle interest in poetry, visit the grave of Robert Frost. An unknown hand has left a small pink geranium beside Emily Dickinson's stone. Just as people throng to see a famous living person pass by, they visit graves to pay their respects to a deceased personage, to feel an intimacy with past achievement, to understand more of the human condition through the evidence of the death that awaits us all.

Perhaps an engraved stone over one's remains represents an effort—a last ditch stand, as it were—to achieve immortality; or sometimes, possibly, an attempt to lay claim to achievement. Witness John A. Joyce and his claim to authorship of "Laugh and the world laughs with you/Weep and you weep alone," forever emblazoned on his monument. Sometimes a granite marker carries a statement about life itself, as does Robert Frost's "I had a lover's quarrel with the world." Sometimes the positioning of the grave carries into death a poignancy that existed in life, such as Louisa May Alcott's being laid beside the other "Little Women" —or a sinister suggestion of questions left unanswered in life, such as Lizzie Borden's being buried above the victims of the axe. Sometimes a grave tells nothing about its occupant's wit, tragedy, daring, or inventiveness; sometimes it can be an awkward, monumental affront to his grace in life, a final irony.

Arnold Toynbee suggests that fame is an attempt to circumvent death. Yet, he points out, it is ironic that the less worthy often achieve fame and immortality because they had bards to record their achievements. Many in these pages had no bard, but they survive in song, legend, custom, or common experience. In these pages we are occasionally irreverent bards, recording their burial places and deeds because they have added shots of color and texture to the peculiarly interwoven American culture.

Sometimes the graves of people who have left their mark on the American scene are passed by, their achievements not forgotten but their names unfamiliar. There was a real mother who had a real daughter who founded Mother's Day. A real person invented the safety pin. Someone really did say "Don't give up the ship!" Whistler had a real father. A real Casey Jones "mounted to his cabin" and took a real "farewell trip to the Promised Land." And a real woman wrote "Mary had a little lamb." We have chosen these, and others, because it was a surprise and a curiosity to discover their identities. We view them through a shifting lens—from today's context to yesterday's.

Although not all the people whose graves are included in this book are well known, some are: Calamity Jane (who knows her by her real name, Martha Jane Cannary Burke?), Horace Greeley, Fannie Farmer, Walt Whitman, Carry Nation, and others equally familiar. John F. Kennedy is *not* included in this book; nor is Abraham Lincoln. Such people have their own bards, and postcards will show you their final resting places. We chose some of the familiar names, such as Messrs. Merrill, Lynch, Pierce, Fenner and Beane, because it struck our fancy to put them back together again, in the same book if not in the same boardroom. Others we chose because we like the manner in which they lived, or died—for example, the manner in which Cole Porter turned his back forever on New York. Some led mysterious lives, or grotesque lives, or noble lives, or, like Eugene O'Neill, haunted lives. Some strode head-on to their deaths, like Diamond Jim Brady, who went to Atlantic City to meet his maker, "the man in the white nightgown." For others, like H. L. Mencken, death was simply a date on time's calendar, because the public voice had stilled long before.

Characters make up any book, and our cast is no exception. The difference is that all our characters are dead—the photographs convey tangible evidence of that. Yet we think their gravestones are touchstones—beyond mere curiosity and a certain macabre appeal—to a lively, living interest in their diverse influences upon us, our heritage, our everyday customs.

Writers of the American Experience

Writers have an edge on immortality. These American authors give us, through their words, a sense of their time and place and therefore our time and place.

Herman Melville

(1819–1891)
AUTHOR

Woodlawn Cemetery
Bronx, New York

Theories about Herman Melville's gravestone, reportedly designed by himself, have popped up frequently ever since his works were rediscovered in the twenties. Often the speculations are as obscure as the Great White Whale itself. Is the blank scroll a cynical commentary on the meaninglessness of a life devoted to writing? Or was it left empty as an invitation to the future to write Melville's name on the scroll of immortal bards? Does the carved stone vine, like the character named Vine in Melville's longest poem, represent Nathaniel Hawthorne, for whom Melville had at least a spiritual passion, an "infinite fraternity of feeling"? Or is the vine-covered sarcophagus a symbolic whale wherein Melville lurks, Jonahlike, waiting to be regurgitated in a frothy resurrection?

Melville lived restlessly, first fathoming the seas and then the inner world for the unfathomable. Occasionally he plunged into metaphysical conversations with his peers and forgot the time. Hawthorne's wife spoke of "his tumultuous waves of thought." He entertained his family and friends with tales of his South Seas adventures, including his capture by benevolent natives on a jungle isle, which he acted out with considerable verve. He wrote in the mornings and customarily walked an hour each day. He tended his fences and barns at his farm in Pittsfield, Massachusetts, where he lived for thirteen years and where he wrote *Moby Dick*.

His first books, accounts of his exotic experiences, brought him instant success and an audience eager for more. But by the time he was thirty and writing *Moby Dick*, his fame caused him to wonder whether fame had any glory or meaning. When his masterpiece was published it was not particularly successful.

He worked as a customs inspector in New York in order to support his wife and four children and to have the freedom to write as he liked. His study-bedroom had an air of sanctified darkness with its black iron bed with dark coverings and books and papers piled in the shadows. A small note pasted alongside his desk, almost out of sight, read, "Keep true to the dreams of thy youth."

Eight months before his death he completed *Billy Budd, Foretopman*, but the manuscript was stored in a breadbox by his widow and daughter and not published until 1924. At the time of his death, forty years after the publication of *Moby Dick*, his books were out of print and the world thought he had already died. His obituary notice was only a few lines long.

Eugene Gladstone O'Neill
(1888–1953)
PLAYWRIGHT

Forest Hills Cemetery
Jamaica Plain, Massachusetts

The inner screams sounding in Eugene O'Neill's work echo the equally ironic and tragic story of his life. His family, portrayed in *Long Day's Journey into Night,* plagued him—one generation, even after death, inflicting its destiny upon the next. The voice of doom cries out in his plays over and over again. O'Neill used his own life and background in his art, struggling to come to grips with it, or to shake off his addiction to the relentless theme of his past. The past contained waste, recrimination, unsatisfied searching. So, it seemed, did the present.

O'Neill's brother was an alcoholic; his older son committed suicide; he was estranged from his daughter and younger son, both of whom he excluded from his will. By 1946 a palsy, diagnosed as Parkinson's disease, made it difficult for him to sign his name. Although he might clutch his right wrist with his left hand in an effort to control his pen, he could no longer pursue his craft. The talent that had earned him four Pulitzer Prizes and a Nobel Prize was crushed by a cruel physical malady.

His relationship with Carlotta, his third wife, was one of love-hate, trust-dread. At one point, when he was hospitalized, he could not bear to see her; yet he always returned to her, and in the shroud of that particular, isolating destiny, spent the last two-and-a-half years of his life with her in a Boston hotel. Shortly before he died, O'Neill half raised himself in bed and cried, "I knew it, I knew it! Born in a goddam hotel room and dying in a hotel room!"

The direct cause of death was bronchial pneumonia. An autopsy showed that only one lung was functional and there was evidence, according to one report, that the palsy resulted from a "familial tremor," a rare inherited condition allayed by alcohol.

Maintaining her role of protectress, Carlotta would not reveal the name of the undertaker or anything about the funeral arrangements. She waited for publicity to die down; as a result, O'Neill was not buried for six days. Then, because word had leaked out, the two-vehicle cortege left at one instead of two in the afternoon, silently and secretly weaving through Boston streets to the cemetery. No old friends were at the graveside.

Eugene O'Neill's stark New England granite stone stands in a sparsely occupied area of the rocky cemetery. But he did not rest in peace immediately: A few days after he was buried, his body had to be moved when it was discovered that the coffin was six inches off the burial plot.

Thomas Clayton Wolfe
(1900–1938)
AUTHOR

Riverside Cemetery
Asheville, North Carolina

Thomas Wolfe's portrayal of his hometown in his first autobiographical novel made him unpopular in Asheville. He missed nothing of life and emotion, he forgot nothing, and he wrote of everything, as if a book were boundless.

His exploring energy seemed boundless as well, but it was not. In the summer of 1938 he made a tour of the Pacific Northwest, where he became seriously ill with pneumonia. In mid-August, after the first siege of illness, he wrote a letter with paper and pen smuggled into his hospital room in Seattle. It was to Maxwell Perkins, his editor and friend. He wrote, in part, "I've made a long voyage and been to a strange country, and I've seen the dark man very close; and I don't think I was too much afraid of him, but so much mortality still clings to me . . ."

It was his last letter. He was sent by train to a Baltimore brain specialist, who found that the cruel headaches Wolfe had suffered were not caused by a tumor or abcess. The pneumonia had reopened an old tuberculosis lesion on his lung, and the infection had spread to his brain. At Johns Hopkins Hospital in September, the surgeon who opened Wolfe's skull in the hope that there might be a removable tuberculoma, simply laid down the scalpel. Wolfe died three days later.

Baltimore did not have a coffin large enough to hold Wolfe's six-foot-seven-inch frame so one was ordered specially from New York. In Asheville, mourners arrived at The Old Kentucky Home, his mother's boardinghouse, to sympathize and to see the writer, with rouged cheeks and tipsy toupee hiding his shaved head, lying in his casket. Did anyone recall the passage about his brother Ben's death, in *Look Homeward, Angel?* There, the undertaker takes a tube of rouge from his pocket, brightens up Ben's coloring and, wholly satisfied, asks, "Did you ever see anything more natural in your life? . . . That's art, boys."

The writer was buried beside his brother Ben and his father, who had been a gravestone carver, in the cemetery he had written about. For it was here that he had the youthful vision, "the wild and secret prophecy," that he would leave the hill-bound town for the "triumphant promise of new lands." He had left, and now he was returned.

Margaret Mitchell Marsh
(1900–1949)
NOVELIST

Oakland Cemetery
Atlanta, Georgia

It took this small, ladylike Georgian, weaned on tales of the Civil War, to convince millions of Yankees that the South had its own brand of grit. A housewife and a reporter on a local Atlanta newspaper, Margaret Mitchell, while confined with an ankle injury, amused herself by starting to piece a novel together. She began by writing the last chapter first; nine years later she had a finished manuscript that filled a suitcase.

Gone With the Wind was her first and only book, and it made her an instant celebrity. The public's assault on her privacy was comparable only to Grant's siege at Vicksburg. Her life became so topsy-turvy that the creator of Scarlett O'Hara and Rhett Butler vowed that she would never write another word. She sold the film rights for fifty thousand dollars with the stipulation that she would in no way be involved with its production. At the Atlanta premiere she became wary when producer David O. Selznick asked about a sequel and didn't give him so much as a fiddle-deedee. She said she just wanted to live a quiet life and grow old in a "fat and amiable" fashion.

But growing old was denied her. One August evening after dining in a cafeteria, she and her husband started to cross Peachtree Street on their way to a movie. Suddenly a speeding car, driven by a drunken off-duty taxi driver, hurtled toward them on the wrong side of the street and struck the diminutive writer. The impact fractured her pelvis in two places and her skull from the top of her head to the top of her spine. She died five days later at the age of only forty-nine.

Engraved invitations admitted friends and relatives to the nine-minute Episcopal service. In a special section of the chapel, reserved for blacks, one of the mourners was a woman who had been Margaret Mitchell's maid for twenty years. The very first bequest in the writer's will was to her: the house that she had been buying from her mistress in weekly payments.

Margaret Mitchell is buried in Atlanta's oldest cemetery, which lies just beyond the area devastated by Sherman's murderous fires, which she depicted so vividly.

John Henry O'Hara
(1905–1970)
WRITER

Princeton Cemetery
Princeton, New Jersey

All his life John O'Hara, the Boswell of America's small-town rich, suffered an almost phobic conviction that he was underrecognized. The popularity of his novels and the royalties he earned were not enough; he sought the trappings of recognition, and when they were not forthcoming he was bitterly stung. With one exception, a National Book Award for *Ten North Frederick*, he never received a major literary prize, although he was nominated at least twice for the Nobel Prize. He angled for honorary degrees, which were never conferred; when asked why not, one university president answered tartly, "because he asked for it."

O'Hara thought it was because he wrote for the lowly. "I have an instinct for what an ordinary guy likes," he rationalized. "It used to hurt never winning an award, but I've never been the pet of intellectuals, the eggheads." But it was not the eggheads and intellectuals who made him a wealthy man and enabled him to build his handsome estate in Princeton and indulge another of his great ambitions—to own a Rolls-Royce. Although slowed by back trouble, difficulty in swallowing, and a diabetic condition, he continued to write to the very end. One spring night (he worked at night and slept during the day) he wrote his last sentence—"Edna had not suspected him, and now his affair with Alicia was a thing of the past"—went to bed, bothered by chest and arm pains, and died of a heart attack in his sleep.

A reporter once asked him, if he were a literary critic, how he would sum up his career. "Better than anyone else," O'Hara replied, "he told the truth about his time, the first half of the Twentieth Century. He is a professional; he wrote honestly and well." Without knowing it, he was writing his own epitaph. The new grave in the picture is his widow's. She was killed several years later in an automobile accident on her way to a party, dressed in a mink jacket and slacks and driving alone in a Mercedes with O'Hara's special plate, "JOH-1."

John Louis Kerouac
(1922–1969)
"BEAT" WRITER

Edson Cemetery
Lowell, Massachusetts

Jack Kerouac batted out the "spontaneous prose" of *On the Road* on a continuous roll of teletype paper in three weeks. Fame did not bring solid literary respect for the man who coined the term "beat generation." The crown he wore as "King of the Beats" was a heavy one, bringing hero worship he did not desire, from hippies who sought him out and lurked like phantoms on his doorstep.

Baptized Jean Louis Lebris de Kerouac, he was called by the diminutive "Ti Jean." The pull of his French roots took Kerouac abroad in search of himself—he spent one of his last trips drunk on cognac in Brittany. His restlessness put him on American highways and the ups and downs of its by-ways. His mother worked in a shoe factory and sent him money when he was broke. When he was home she kept house for him, chose the middle-class furnishings for the small house he bought, and shooed away his friends when she found them unpleasant. In 1966, when drinking had taken over his life, she took comfort in the fact that a crucifix hung over his bed, as if it established his essential innocence.

After she had a stroke, Kerouac took his mother to Florida for her health. Bothered by a hernia, he shuttled between working on a chronicle of his helter-skelter life and alternating between slugs of whiskey and gulps of beer. One evening, after an attack of vomiting, he was taken to the hospital, where he died of a massive internal hemorrhage.

His body was laid out at a mortuary in Lowell. Someone placed rosary beads on his clasped hands. A handful of his "beat" friends, beads of a different kind dangling around their necks, attended the Roman Catholic service and shuffled along with the small group of mourners to the cemetery.

Children's Writers

Children form their ambitions, their views of good and bad, their dreams, through what they read. These authors inculcated generations of children with the American notion of being able to have your head in the clouds—so long as your feet are on the ground.

Louisa May Alcott
(1832–1888)
AUTHOR

Sleepy Hollow Cemetery
Concord, Massachusetts

No writer of today would dare to have one child, make-believe or not, say to another, "My Danny tooked tare of me all day, and I was dood." And Mark Twain had a field day with heroines who evaded lovers with such lines as, "Dear Mac, I cannot give you the love you want, but I trust and respect you from the bottom of my heart, if that is any comfort."

Louisa May Alcott's work is sprinkled with this kind of nineteenth-century sentimentality. But, behind the world of saccharine goodness, innocent pranks, and absolute purity of soul, was an author firmly rooted in practicality. Louisa May wrote because she had to. She was the family breadwinner, whose money, earned from her popular books, bought the family home in Concord, Massachusetts, and supported her mother, father, and siblings. When she was thirty-six, with twenty more years of life and toil ahead of her, she wrote in her journal, "Paid up all the debts—thank the Lord!—every penny that money can pay—and now I feel as if I could die in peace."

This frail woman—typhoid fever caught while doing Civil War hospital work had weakened her—was the daughter of a dreamer father, whom she looked after until she died. In 1885, she bought a house on Boston's Beacon Hill, but she could not stay there with her father, for she was suffering from headaches, vertigo, and stomach pains. She went to the country for a "rest and milk" cure, but gradually grew worse. In March 1888 she went to visit her dying father, caught cold, became unconscious, and died—unaware of his death two days before her own.

The simple service she had wanted took place in the Boston house. Her body then was carried to Concord and laid in the family plot. Her small stone, bearing only the initials L.M.A. and her dates, is the first in a row containing her sisters' graves— almost as if a strange performance of *Little Women* were about to begin, with the ending known. Directly behind her is the larger gravestone of her nephew, John Sewall Pratt Alcott, whom, in her pragmatic way, she had adopted, so that she would have a direct legal heir to inherit her copyrights.

Horatio Alger, Jr.

(1832–1899)
AUTHOR

Glenwood Cemetery
South Natick, Massachusetts

It is hard to imagine anyone more unlike a Horatio Alger hero than Horatio Alger himself. Small and self-effacing, giving the appearance of a man just leaving the room, Alger was the very antithesis of the ruddy, self-assured, rags-to-riches young men who adorned his novels. What is more, his private life was such that, if he had modeled his heroes after himself, instead of after his fancies, his books would have been sold in plain wrappers under the counter, instead of openly in the millions of copies that made him the most popular author of his generation.

A spurious "biography" of Alger, later unmasked as a literary hoax, is responsible for his widely accepted reputation as a womanizer. If the author had stuck to the truth, the story would have been just as spicy. The son of a rock-ribbed minister and an over-protective mother, Alger grew up in a straitjacket of New England piety and was nicknamed "Holy Horatio" by his schoolmates. He graduated from Harvard Divinity School and, in 1864, received a call to become minister of the Unitarian church at Brewster, Massachusetts. His fifteen months there in the service of the Lord were abruptly terminated when two parish boys revealed that the Reverend Mr. Alger had been buggering them. Alger did not deny the charge; he left town the same day, and a discreet word to Unitarian headquarters put an end to his pastoral career forever.

It was the turning point in Alger's life, but not an unwelcome one, since his real aspiration was to be a writer, and he had already achieved something of a literary reputation. Staying in New England was out of the question, so he moved to New York. Within two years he had published his first successful novel, *Ragged Dick*, followed by an avalanche of others. The theme was always the same: An attractive young man makes good against heavy odds. It may be wondered whether his preoccupation with attractive young men was not limited to the printed page, but after the Brewster episode there was never again a breath of scandal involving his name.

In his later years, asthma and bronchitis plagued him; and he lived in the constant fear that he would develop pneumonia. One summer day in 1899, he struggled out of bed to try to write, but was too weak to reach the table. Gently, his sister led him back to bed and said, "You've written enough, Horatio." His publisher put it as well as any: "What Alger has done is to portray the soul—the ambitious soul—of the country."

Poets

These poets dealt with uniquely American themes. They opened spiritual doors to fresh perceptions of the American identity.

James Russell Lowell
(1819–1891)

POET, TEACHER, ESSAYIST, DIPLOMAT

Mount Auburn Cemetery
Cambridge, Massachusetts

If Emily Dickinson was a very private poet, James Russell Lowell was a very public one. He lived in the mainstream of American intellectual life. As well as being a composer of verse ("What is so rare as a day in June?"), he was a teacher of modern languages at Harvard, an editor of the *Atlantic Monthly* and of the *North American Review,* a minister to Spain and Great Britain, an essayist who inveighed against slavery long before the Civil War. He was, in truth, the epitome of the man of letters, and a very sociable one at that. He never understood Thoreau, whose views about the solitary life made him uneasy.

One day, when Lowell was seventy, he and a friend passed a home for "incurable children." That, Lowell pointed out, was where he would be sent. He did not feel old, despite attacks of gout. Nevertheless, not long after this gentle joke at himself, Lowell became ill from what seemed to be kidney trouble. During the ensuing year he continued to read and reread old favorites—among them Boswell and Milton—and even popular novels; and to receive visitors in his study at his home, Elmwood, next door to the Longfellow house in Cambridge.

The passing months brought the trials of a weakening body—nausea, sleeplessness, coughing, and pain. The kidney trouble turned out to be cancer, which spread. Lowell wasn't interested in a label for his illness. "What will be, will be," he said. Finally opium drugged the pain. When conscious, he worried about the bother he was causing his daughter, and without rancor asked, "Why don't you let me die?" When he did, in his own room at Elmwood, those attending him did not realize at first that his breathing had stopped.

The funeral service at Harvard was as plain as possible. Dr. Oliver Wendell Holmes was among the pallbearers. Church bells tolled as the burial party moved from the chapel toward the cemetery. There, Longfellow, who had died nine years earlier, would again be his neighbor, but with a grand tomb approached by steps suggesting perpetual reverence. Lowell had said, "I fancy an honest man easier in his grave with the bare truth told about him on his headstone." And so the New England Puritan slate, unusual as late as 1891, records the simplest of human facts.

Walter (Walt) Whitman

(1819–1892)
POET

Harleigh Cemetery
Camden, New Jersey

Whitman abbreviated the "Walter" in his name in 1855, when his first edition of *Leaves of Grass* appeared. From that time on he was to be the self-proclaimed spokesman for the proletariat. He took the stance of the working man: noble, democratic, strong, formed by and forming this land. In his poetry, he wrote of the "cheerful voice of the public road"; and he took, vagabondlike, to this "open road"—"to eat and sleep with the earth." Whitman celebrated life and proclaimed the dignity of the common man and of man-made structures: pavements, bridges, ferries, stone and steel city buildings.

The people about whom he wrote were massive, beautiful, healthy, and independent; but their poet was only mortal. In 1873, at the age of fifty-four, Whitman suffered a stroke that left him partially paralyzed for the rest of his life, which he spent, writing and revising his work, in Camden, New Jersey. In 1888, his body was dealt another blow by another stroke. In addition, the pains in his abdomen, chest, and ankles did not subside, nor did a persistent hiccup. An autopsy revealed that his body was totally ravaged by tuberculosis.

The poet of democracy had arranged, at notable expense, for the construction of the mausoleum where his body lies. And the poet of the people has been visited by the people, as the graffiti on surrounding trees show. Behind the iron railing at the entrance, a few discarded chewing-gum wrappers lie on the damp ground.

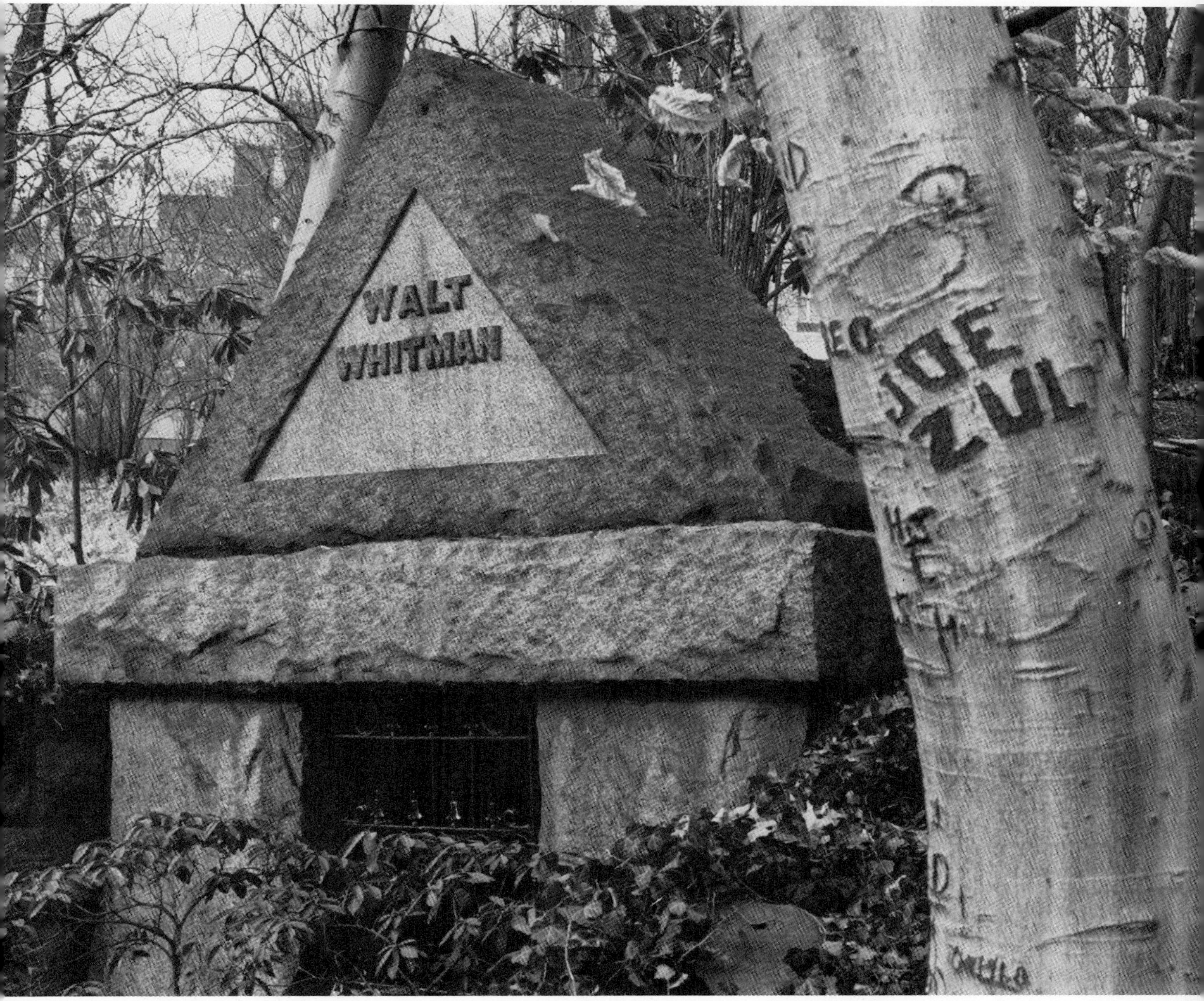
WALT
WHITMAN
JOE
ZUL

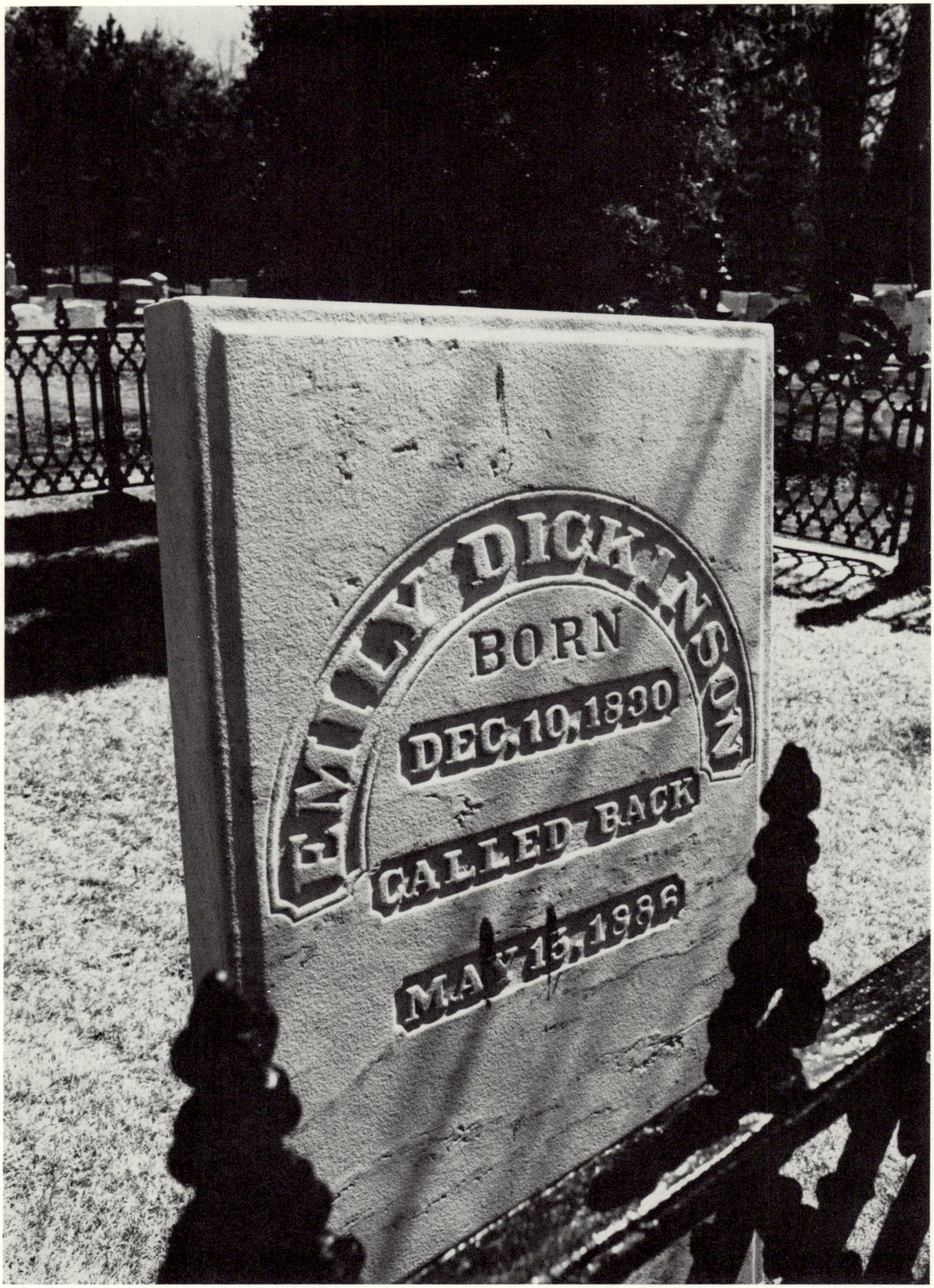
EMILY DICKINSON
BORN
DEC. 10, 1830
CALLED BACK
MAY 15, 1886

Emily Elizabeth Dickinson
(1830–1886)
POET

West Cemetery
Amherst, Massachusetts

Emily Dickinson's reputation as a major innovative poet has been surrounded by as much controversy as the great clouds of ectoplasm that obscure what little is known of her personal life. Her life as a recluse is supposed to have been the result of a hopeless love affair with a married man. The publication of a handful of her letters, suppressed for almost seventy years, written to Judge Otis Phillips Lord of Salem (a close friend and contemporary of her father) after his wife's death, points the finger of suspicion at the doorstep, or perhaps the chambers, of a leading member of the Massachusetts judiciary. The highly erotic content of some of these letters suggests that Judge Lord's frequent visits to Amherst may not have been devoted wholly to the ministration of justice, and when read in conjunction with Emily's three mysterious "Master" letters, written many years earlier, suggests the existence of an affair with her "Lord and Master" even during Mrs. Lord's lifetime.

For whatever reason, Emily withdrew in her early thirties to the seclusion of her father's household. She dressed entirely in white; ventured away from the grounds only once to flit around a new church on a moonlit night; and spent most of her time in her room composing the neatly stitched packets, written in a tiny, almost undecipherable hand, which were found in a bureau drawer after her death. Often the unconventional and eccentric poetry seems to reflect glimpses of conflict between heavenly poems and earthly desires, repressed perhaps by devotion to a dominant father and loyalty to family and virginity. Out of nearly eighteen hundred poems, only seven were published during her lifetime.

During her years of seclusion, no one outside Emily's immediate family ever laid eyes on her. Occasionally, she would "receive" visitors while standing out of sight in a darkened hallway, whispering to them around the corner as they sat in the lighted parlor, uneasily sipping tea. Once, when she was ill, even the doctor was not permitted to examine her but was obliged to diagnose and prescribe while standing outside her bedroom door. Only after her death were a select few permitted to view her frail white-clad body, a privilege none had enjoyed during her lifetime.

Her last known letter, written to two relatives of whom she was especially fond, said simply, "Little Cousins, Called Back, Emily." Still faintly visible on her worn marble stone are the words, "Called Back."

Robert Lee Frost
(1874–1963)
POET

First Congregational Church Cemetery
Old Bennington, Vermont

The direct tone in the verses of America's best-loved pastoral poet belies a troubled and sometimes angry soul, whose private life was fraught with sorrows: a baby boy who lived but a day; another son who died in his fourth year; a daughter who died in childbirth; another daughter who became a chronic invalid; and a devoted wife, who died of a heart attack after forty years of marriage, and left him a widower for another twenty-five.

Yet these inner sorrows are scarcely evident in the timeless treasure of poetry he left to his country. More than any other poet, he symbolized the rough-hewn individuality of the American creative spirit. It was, perhaps, because of the contrast that his pathetic appearance at the Kennedy inauguration—a frail old man, who found himself unable to read the lines he had written for the occasion—made such a moving impression on the millions who were watching. The following year he fainted in Grand Central Terminal and shortly thereafter underwent surgery in Boston. Even after a heart attack and a second operation for removal of blood clots, he continued to receive a steady stream of friends in the hospital, from college presidents to railroad porters, some of whom he persuaded to smuggle oysters and shrimp into his room while the nurse was on her lunch break. He weakened progressively, and toward the end began to stare at the bedside clock, as if marking time. He died suddenly and peacefully of a pulmonary embolism.

His epitaph, expressly written as such, is from his poem "The Lesson for Today"; his wife's, from "The Master Speed."

ROBERT LEE FROST
MAR. 26, 1874 — JAN. 29, 1963
"I HAD A LOVER'S QUARREL WITH THE WORLD."

HIS WIFE
ELINOR MIRIAM WHITE
OCT. 25, 1873 — MAR. 20, 1938
"TOGETHER WING TO WING AND OAR TO OAR."

They Live Through a Line or Two

There are those who live through a line or two, in phrases or simple verses, which Americans know instinctively but never ponder. These men and women led full lives but they are forgotten except for a few words, which by happenstance go on without them.

In memory of
CAPTAIN JAMES LAWRENCE
of the United States Navy

James Lawrence

(1781–1813)
NAVAL OFFICER

Trinity Churchyard
New York, New York

>   The HEROIC COMMANDER
>   of the frigate Chesapeake,
>   whose remains are here deposited
>   expressed with his dying breath
>   his devotion to his Country.
>   Neither the fury of battle,
>   the anguish of a mortal wound,
>   nor the horrors of approaching death,
>   could subdue his gallant Spirit
>   His dying words were
>   DON'T GIVE UP THE SHIP

James Lawrence might never have said the stirring last words he lives by, had he not fatally misjudged the frigate *Shannon* as a sitting duck for an attack. A letter from its British captain, challenging Lawrence to a battle at any latitude and longitude of his choice, had never been received. So Lawrence set sail from Boston Harbor on his frigate *Chesapeake*, with a green crew, determined to whomp the *Shannon* where she lay. Within minutes after the first gun was fired, Lawrence, standing on the quarterdeck in full dress uniform, was shot. "DON'T GIVE UP THE SHIP!" he wheezed, as they carted him below. A one-armed British boat-swain lashed the two ships together and the enemy swarmed aboard, overwhelming the American crew, which simply fled. The *Chesapeake* struck her colors and Lawrence was dead.

The British captain was made a baronet, but nobody remembers what *he* said. Lawrence lies buried in New York's financial district, and everybody knows what *he* said. But we wonder why his dying words became a rallying cry, a symbol of naval courage, when "give up the ship" was exactly what they did.

Sarah Josepha Buell Hale

(1788–1879)
EDITOR, WRITER

Laurel Hill Cemetery
Philadelphia, Pennsylvania

>Mary had a little lamb
>Its fleece was white as snow
>And everywhere that Mary went
>The lamb was sure to go.

"Mary's Lamb" first appeared in 1830 in *Juvenile Miscellany*, published in Boston, above the initials S.J.H. It was subsequently included in a children's songbook. But its presence (unsigned) in *McGuffey's Reader* assured its place in national folklore through the thousands of children who used the primer in American elementary schools.

Writing nursery rhymes was not Sarah Hale's primary endeavor. For fifty years she was editor and overseer of *Godey's Lady's Book*, the most influential women's periodical of her day, through which she encouraged women to educate themselves and to assert their "mental powers." She also wrote thirty-six books and conducted intensive campaigns for reform in education and in the penal system.

Throughout all of this extraordinary activity, Mrs. Hale was periodically obliged to defend her authorship of one small slip of a poem against the opportunists who claimed it as their own. One was a Mrs. Mary Tyler who, in 1878, pulled out some old wool stockings, said that they had been made from her little lamb's fleece—presumably after he had followed her to school—and that a Harvard student had written the poem about her and the lamb in 1816. Mrs. Tyler unraveled the stockings and sold the wool on little souvenir cards.

"Mary's Lamb" was widely parodied. At one point, Godey himself threw in the sponge and caused his final comment to be printed in his *Lady's Book:*

>Mary had a little lamb
>'Twas subject to the gout,
>At last she got disgusted,
>And put it up the spout.

Sarah Hale retired as editor at the age of eighty-nine, only sixteen months before her death. She spent most of her last months in her room, surrounded by caged singing birds, illustrious visitors, and grandchildren at play. A few days before she died, she dictated a letter asserting for the last time her authorship of "Mary's Lamb." Then, one April evening, she fell asleep and slipped quietly into death.

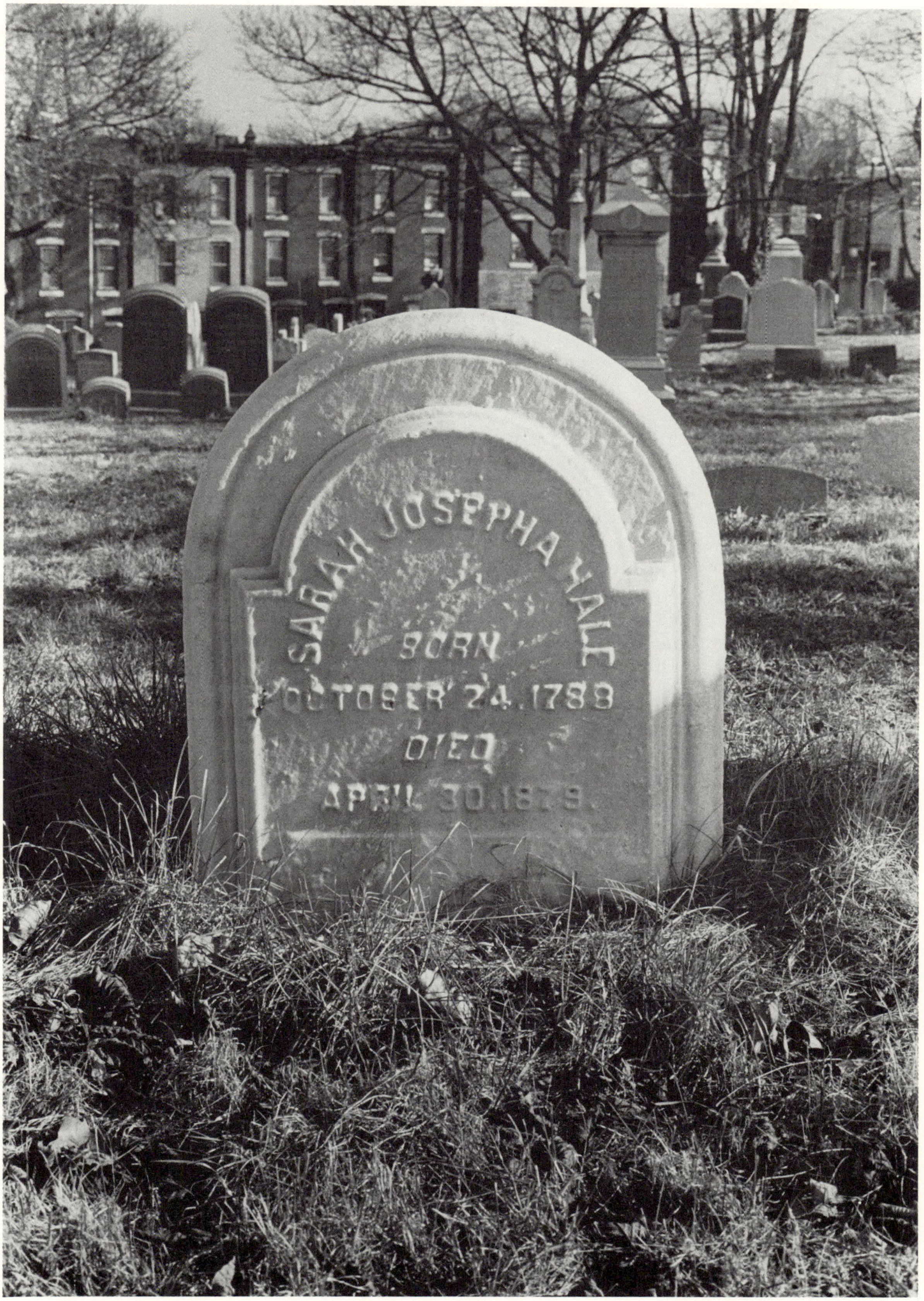
SARAH JOSEPPHA HALE
BORN
OCTOBER 24. 1788
DIED
APRIL 30. 1879

Horace Greeley

(1811–1872)

JOURNALIST, REFORMER, POLITICIAN

Green-Wood Cemetery
Brooklyn, New York

In 1872, Horace Greeley, founder and editor of the New York *Tribune*, ran against incumbent Ulysses S. Grant for the presidency of the United States. The campaign was bitter and humiliating; it left Greeley financially, physically, and emotionally unstable. His wife died shortly before the election and Greeley less than a month after.

Greeley's demise was an event such as Currier and Ives often depicted, with several luminaries hovering in the room, awaiting the end. Whitelaw Reid, who recently had wrested control of the *Tribune* from Greeley, was deputized to approach the deathbed and hear the great man's last words. Greeley came to for a moment, recognized Reid and growled, "You son of a bitch, you stole my newspaper." Reid retreated from the bedside and the others crowded around to hear Greeley's last message. "His last words," Reid solemnly reported, "were 'I know my redeemer liveth.' "

One of Greeley's many crusades had been in support of free homesteading. In this context he made famous some words of advice: "Go West, young man," he urged, "go West."

The bust atop Horace Greeley's grave faces east.

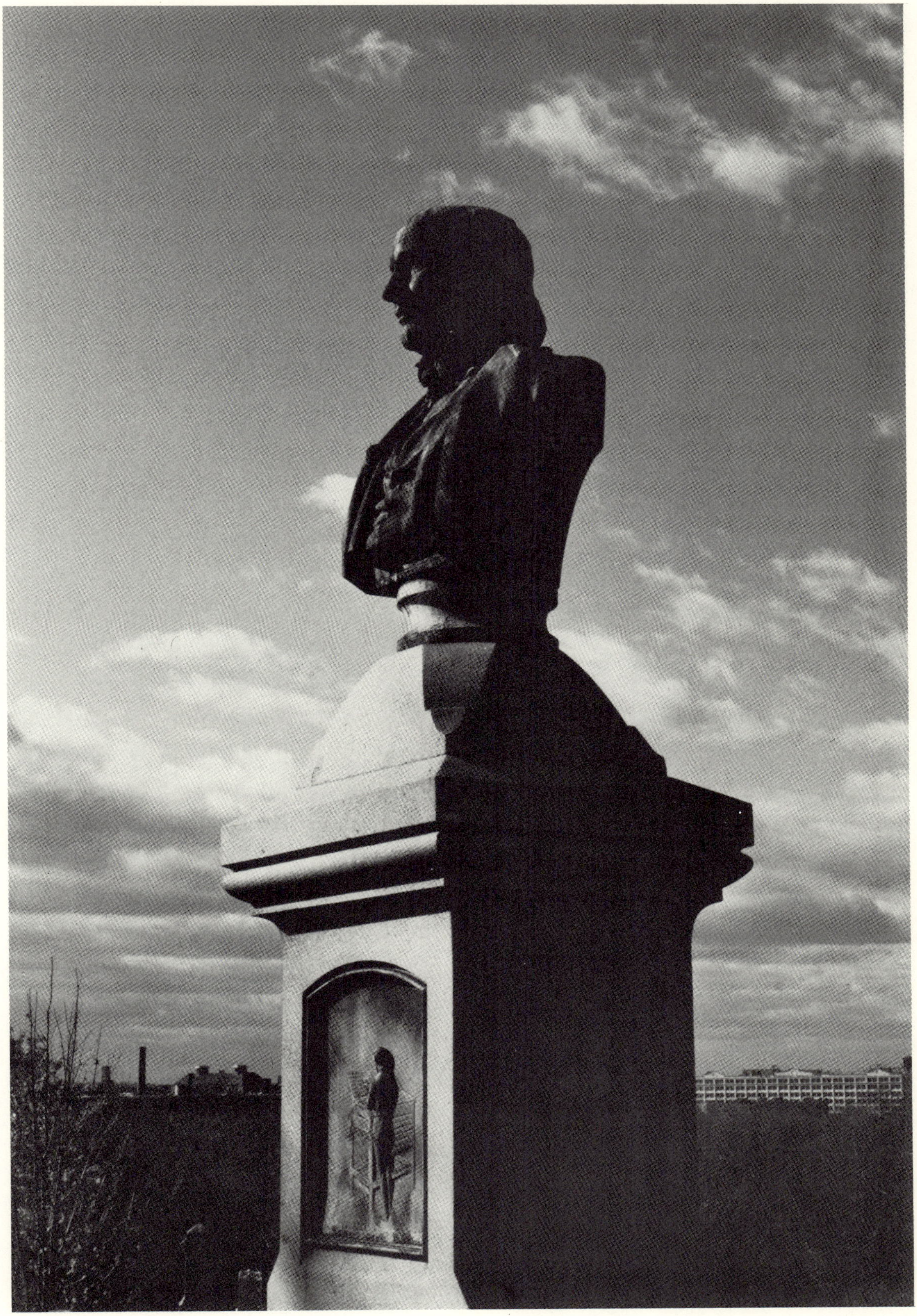

John A. Joyce
(1842–1915)
POET

Oak Hill Cemetery
Washington, D.C.

Who wrote "Laugh and the world laughs with you/Weep and you weep alone"? John A. Joyce, self-proclaimed author, had to wrangle with a "poetess of passion" over this oft-quoted verse. The former soldier, dubbed "Colonel" as a result of service in Kentucky, was a robust skirmisher.

Ella Wheeler Wilcox (1850–1919) published the poem as her own in 1883, calling it "Solitude." Joyce published it as "Love and Laughter" in 1885, but later produced affidavits from Washington cronies saying that they had heard him recite it much earlier.

The poetess recalled the inspiration for her poem: her white dress as she was off to a gala event, and the contrasting sight of a sad woman in widow's weeds. The poet countered with the vivid recollection that he composed the poem while sitting on a whiskey barrel. Joyce gave out autographed copies and quoted "his" poem persistently. Mrs. Wilcox offered a bounty to anyone who could produce a version published before hers.

As the argument waxed more than it waned, Joyce drove another stake in his claim. First he ordered a striking bust of himself carved and set upon his future monument. Then he had the first two lines of "Love and Laughter" engraved on the stone, with his signature below. Finally, he posed, patting the monument for the photographers, and sent off prints of the picture to all his friends with this verse inscribed on the back:

> Spread golden flowers upon my life,
> And do so very often—
> I need them in my daily life
> But not upon my coffin.

And so it went. The poetess outlived the soldier-poet by four years, during which time she lectured to soldiers in France on sexual problems, gave poetry readings, and tried to communicate with her dead husband.

Did Joyce win the last round? Maybe so. His monument, above busy Rock Creek Parkway on one side and the quiet streets of Georgetown on the other, exudes an air of confidence among the neighboring graves of Washington statesmen.

Bravado sometimes carries beyond the grave.

TRUTH
NATUR
JUSTICE
SCIENCE
JOHN A. JOYCE
POET, SOLDIER, PHILOSOPHER.
BORN JULY 4, 1842
DIED JAN. 18, 1915
Laugh and the world laughs with you
Weep and you weep alone.
JOYCE

Where Would We Be Without . . .

Where would we be without the safety pin and the American mom? These people represent American inventiveness at its best—or, maybe not at its worst, but as proof that almost anything might go.

Samuel Finley Breese Morse

(1791–1872)
INVENTOR

Green-Wood Cemetery
Brooklyn, New York

In 1844, when Samuel F. B. Morse sent the world's first telegraphic message—"What hath God wrought!"—one of his assistants explained the invention this way: "Suppose you stretch a dog from Washington to Baltimore. If you step on the dog's tail in Washington, he will yelp in Baltimore. Well, the telegraph responds in Baltimore to something done in Washington. However, it's a lot easier to lay a telegraph wire than it is to stretch a dog." Thus the telegraph ushered in the dog-goned age of instantaneous communication.

If Morse had never heard of electromagnetism he would have continued as an artist. He was already a well-known painter, while his experiments with the daguerreotype drew students, such as Mathew Brady, who flocked to his New York studio to learn the fledgling art of photography. Even before the first wires were buzzing, Morse wrote that he wished "to relieve myself of the cares of the Telegraph" in order to pursue his beloved art. But disputes over the development, ownership, and origin of the device continued, and he did not paint one picture during the last thirty years of his life.

He was writing a response to an "atrocious & absurd" attack when neuralgic pains compelled him to stop. Pneumonia weakened him further, and when the doctor, tapping his chest, said, "This is the way we doctors telegraph," Morse whispered, "Very good." He smiled after that but it was his last message.

In the international code that bears his name the small stone marking his grave would read simply $\cdots / \cdot - \cdot / - \cdots / - - /$.

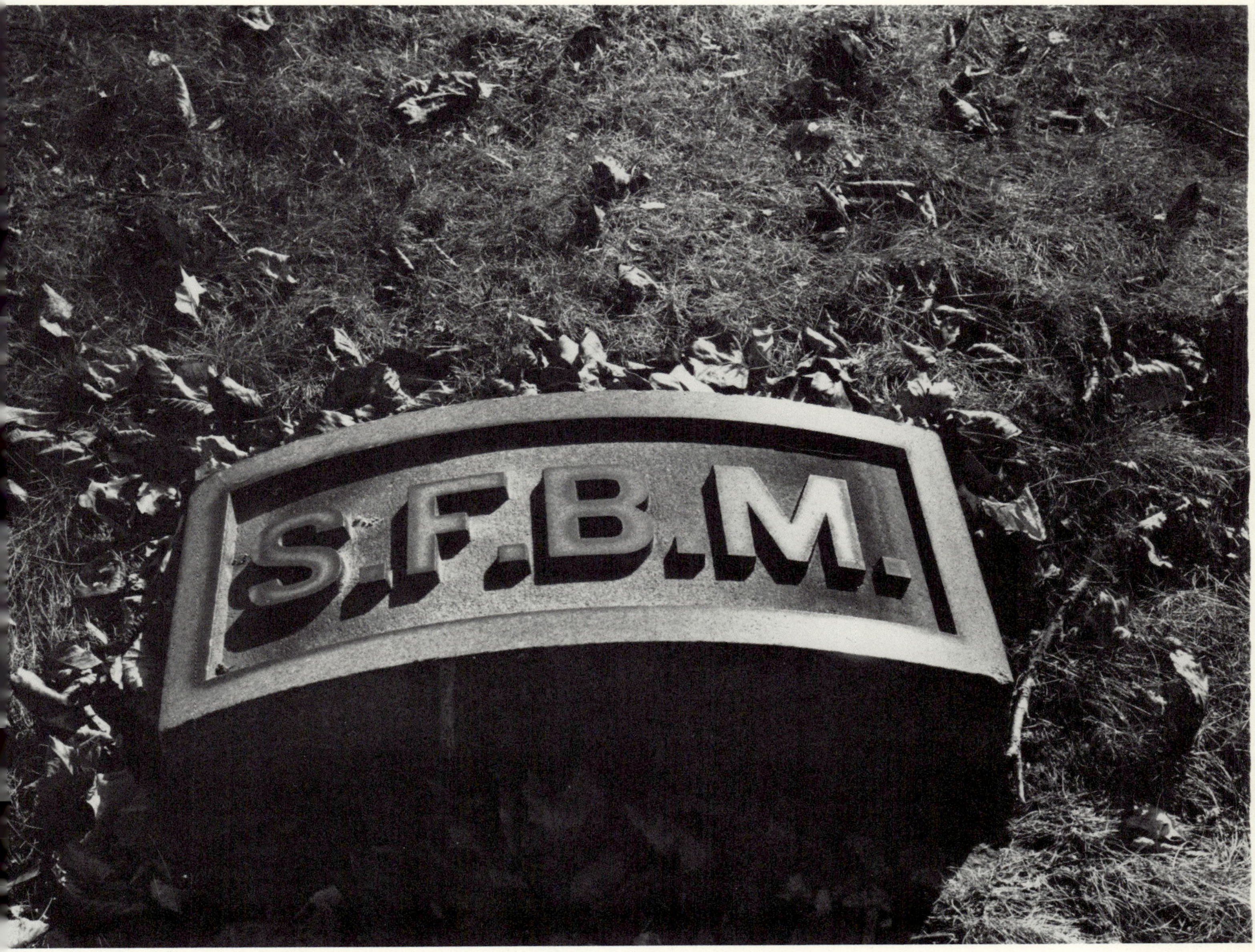
S.F.B.M.

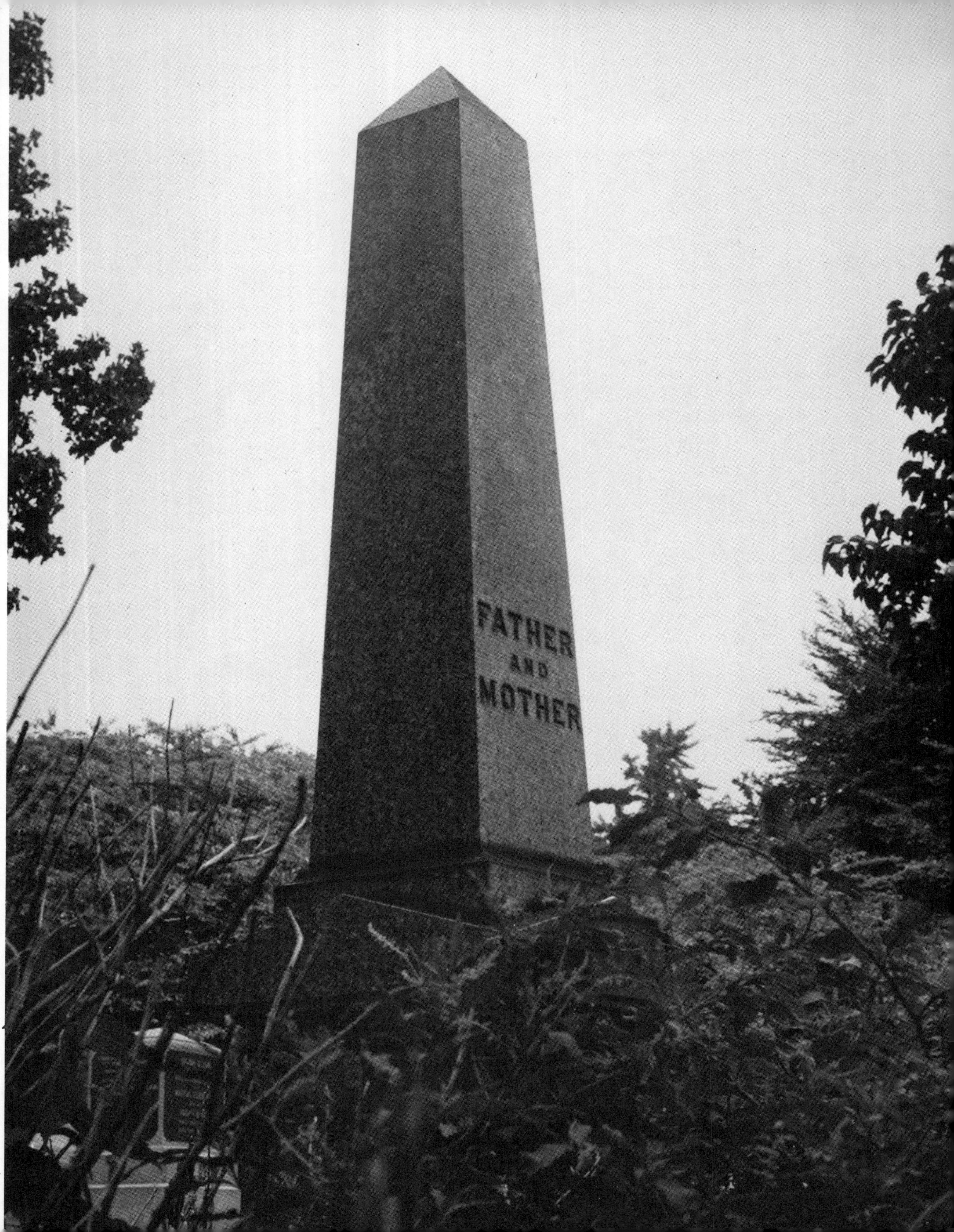
FATHER
AND
MOTHER

Walter Hunt

(1796–1859)
INVENTOR OF THE SAFETY PIN

Green-Wood Cemetery
Brooklyn, New York

Walter Hunt was a Quaker with a fertile mind, and he invented lots of things—a flax-spinning machine, a machine for making boxes from paper pulp, an icebreaker boat, a sewing machine, a fountain pen, a self-closing inkwell, an iron gong for streetcars, and suction shoes that enabled acrobats to walk on ceilings. In his office, one morning in 1849, he started fiddling with a little piece of wire. Three hours later he had invented the modern safety pin. He sold his rights for four hundred bucks, which is all he ever made from it.

Hunt died of pneumonia, and two days later, after a funeral at his daughter's home, he was buried in the family plot. His name is as obscure today as his name on the base of the monument, now covered by overgrown plantings. But without him we would be undone.

Henry (Harry) Wright

(1835–1895)
FATHER OF BASEBALL

West Laurel Hill Cemetery
Bala Cynwyd, Pennsylvania

How did an Englishman who played cricket come to be known as the father of American baseball? Harry Wright's sobriquet may be open to some dispute, but he is generally credited with being the first person to recognize that a ball club could make a living from its gate receipts; and it might perhaps be more accurate to characterize him as the father of *professional* baseball. Another major contribution he made to the game was the official scoring system, still in use today.

Uncle Harry, as everybody called him, was born in England but came to this country as a small boy and became prominent as a cricket player. In 1866, he took a job as an instructor and bowler at the Union Cricket Club in Cincinnati, where he subsequently organized what became the Cincinnati Red Stockings, the first regular professional baseball team in the country. Wright was manager and captain and played pitcher and center field, once making seven home runs in one game. Easily the roughest and toughest bunch of thugs in the slam-bang sport that was baseball in its infancy, Wright's team ravaged the competition like a swarm of red-gaitered locusts in the 1869 and 1870 seasons, winning eighty-seven consecutive games and racking up such scores as thirty-to-eleven, one-hundred-and-three-to-eight, and eighty-to-five, scores unheard of today.

In 1871, the Red Stockings having disbanded, Wright brought both the hose and the name to the newly organized Boston club. Later, he served as manager of the Providence and Philadelphia clubs and as head of the National League staff of umpires, a position he held until his death. He and his brother George, a shortstop, who was also president of the sporting-goods firm of Wright & Ditson, are the only brothers elected to the National Baseball Hall of Fame.

Uncle Harry died of pneumonia at a sanitarium in Atlantic City, after an illness of three weeks. His death was mourned throughout the leagues. Baltimore sent a bank of flowers to the funeral, Brooklyn sent an eight-foot-high lyre of red roses, and Washington a cross of white pinks. Wright's son, whose hands were said to closely resemble those of his father, posed for this statue, which was erected by a group of baseball lovers.

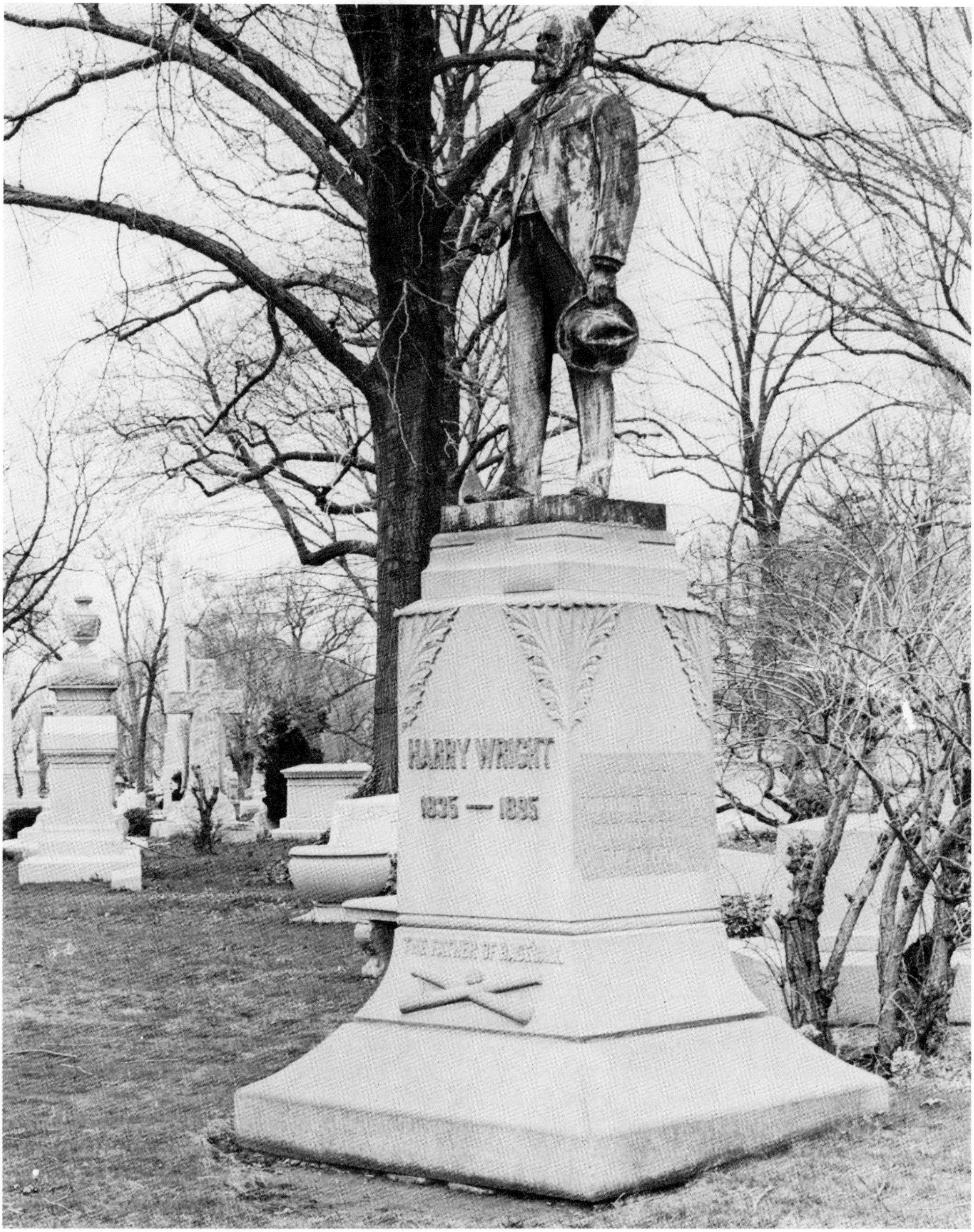
HARRY WRIGHT
1835 — 1895
THE FATHER OF BASEBALL

ANN REEVES
JARVIS
SEPT. 30. 1834
MAY 9. 1905
MOTHER
OF
MOTHER'S DAY
JARVIS
ANNA M. JARVIS
MAY 1. 1864 — NOV. 24. 1948
FOUNDED MOTHER'S DAY MAY. 10. 1908
OFFICIALLY PROCLAIMED BY PRESIDENT
WOODROW WILSON. MAY 9. 1914

ANNA M. JARVIS FOUNDER of MOTHER'S DAY
B. MAY 1 1864
D. NOV 24 1948
PHILADELPHIA. PA. 1908

Anna M. Jarvis
(1864–1948)
FOUNDER OF MOTHER'S DAY

West Laurel Hill Cemetery
Bala Cynwyd, Pennsylvania

Anna M. Jarvis's mother, Mrs. Ann Reeves Jarvis, died on May 9, 1905. On the first anniversary of her mother's death, Anna Jarvis gathered together some friends for a memorial meeting. On the second anniversary she held a church service. Before long, she had embarked on a major crusade, writing to governors, legislators, editors, even to the White House, to gain support for having a day set apart each year in honor of motherhood. Within six years after her mother's death, Mother's Day was observed in almost every state, and on the ninth anniversary, May 9, 1914, it gained national recognition when President Wilson signed a Congressional resolution formally setting aside the second Sunday of May for its observance.

For the rest of her life, Anna Jarvis fought bitterly against the commercialization of Mother's Day. She denounced the practice of buying cards instead of writing letters. She accused florists and candy manufacturers of gouging the public by pandering to sentimentality. At first, she promoted the custom of wearing a carnation on Mother's Day, red if Mother was living, white if she was dead. When the price of carnations soared as a result, she adopted a celluloid button, which she manufactured and distributed without profit to churches, schools, and other organizations.

In time, her correspondence in promoting and defending Mother's Day grew so voluminous that she was obliged to purchase the house next door to store her papers. She exhausted her modest inheritances in these efforts, and eventually, almost blind, she was admitted to a Philadelphia hospital. When friends heard of her plight, they formed a committee and raised funds for her support. Later, she was transferred to a sanitarium near Philadelphia, where she died—deaf, blind, and broke.

Their Names Are Everyday Words

The world of commerce has given us people who are themselves forgotten, but whose names are everyday words. Imagine living on as a cough drop!

Lydia Estes Pinkham

(1819–1883)

PATENT MEDICINE PROPRIETOR

Oak Grove Cemetery
Lynn, Massachusetts

> Oh we sing of Lydia Pinkham
> And her love for the human race.
> She invented the Vegetable Compound
> And the label bears her face.

What is most interesting about Lydia Pinkham is that she did not get into the business that made her name a household word until the very end of her life, and that it was born not as some entrepreneurial brainchild but as a practical means of supporting her semi-invalid husband.

Lydia Estes grew up in middle-class New England respectability, married Isaac Pinkham of New Hampshire, and spent the next three decades raising a family and tending house. She liked to fuss around the kitchen with herbs and roots and, at some point, she came across a formula in *The American Dispensatory,* a forerunner of the U.S. *Pharmacopoeia,* for a "vegetable compound," which she brewed and passed among her lady friends. After sipping the compound (merely twenty percent alcohol), those who suffered from "woman's weakness" did seem to feel more cheery.

In 1873, just after the Pinkhams celebrated their thirtieth wedding anniversary, a financial panic wiped them out. Isaac's health was failing and, after two years in straitened circumstances, they hit on the idea of manufacturing Mother's tonic to bring in some money. The kitchen became a factory, and their sons became salesmen. Their early profits were plowed back into vast numbers of printed flyers and a barrage of newspaper advertisements. It has been said that Lydia Pinkham's Vegetable Compound was the first product to demonstrate the effectiveness of mass marketing, and Mrs. Pinkham's portrait on the label was the first photograph to be used in advertising.

Mrs. Pinkham solicited and received letters from women all over the world, who revealed the innermost secrets of their woes under the guarantee of strict confidence. She answered every letter personally. Later, she wrote the first sex manual to be widely circulated.

Two days before Christmas 1882, Mrs. Pinkham was taken with a paralytic stroke, which affected her speech. For a time she seemed to improve; and her bed was moved into the living room, where she was able to enjoy the company of her family and friends, especially her medium, in whom she took great comfort. She lingered for less than five months and died peacefully.

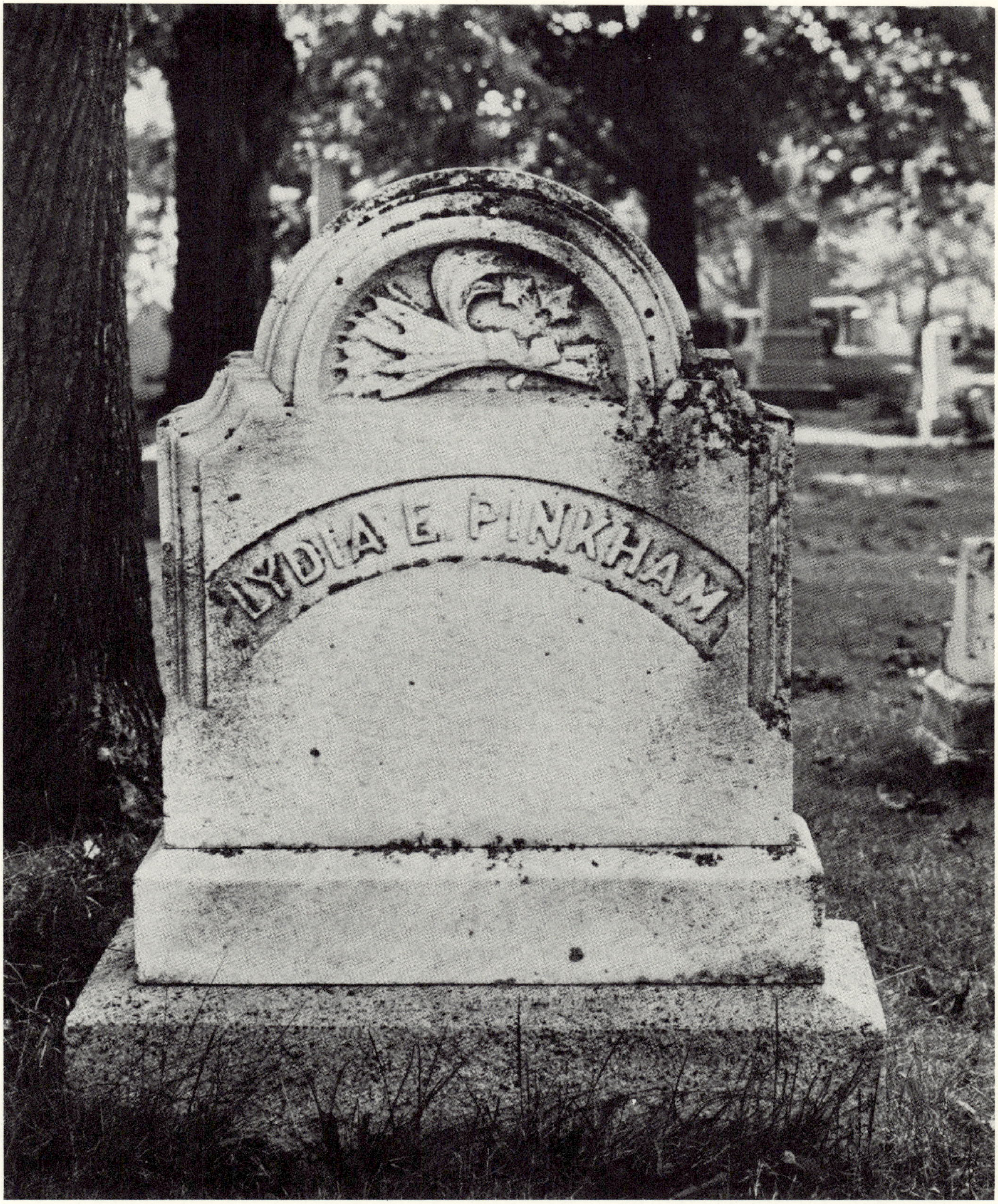
LYDIA E. PINKHAM

William Wallace Smith
(1830–1913)

Andrew Smith
(1836–1895)

THE SMITH BROTHERS

Poughkeepsie Rural Cemetery
Poughkeepsie, New York

When Smith Brothers, Inc., celebrated its centennial in 1947, the current generation of brothers grew beards for the occasion. They were ballyhooed in the press and at commemorative banquets, one of which featured a half grapefruit with a black cough drop in the center. Once the festivities were over, they shaved their faces and retired into the five o'clock shadows of the original brothers, William and Andrew Smith.

James Smith, a Scot, settled in Poughkeepsie, New York, in 1847 and opened a restaurant and candy store. Tradition has it that he purchased a recipe for cough drops from a peddler named Sly Hawkins, and began to market them under the name of James Smith & Sons Compound of Wild Cherry Cough Candy. When he died, in 1866, his two sons, William and Andrew, took over the business. Their likenesses were pasted on the glass bowls from which the lozenges were first dispensed. Within a few years, imitations sprang up—Schmid Brothers, Schmidt Brothers, Schmitt Brothers, Original Smith Brothers, Improved Smith Brothers (some of which featured bearded pictures of Presidents Lincoln, Grant or Garfield), Smyth Brothers (which used pictures of the real brothers), and even a brand called Smith Sisters—so numerously that William and Andrew, shrewdly figuring that their faces were unique, even if their name was not, decided to register themselves as a trademark. Their positioning on the box, with William over TRADE and Andrew over MARK, soon earned for them the nicknames that stuck to them like gooey cough drops ever after.

Mark was an easy-going bachelor, such a soft touch that wags called him Easy Mark, and was known to flesh out his whiskers with the hair of the dog now and then. He died in 1895. Trade, a staunch teetotaler and prohibitionist, probably never knew that one of the principal uses of his product was to disguise alcoholic breath. He ran the business with tight-fisted Scottish frugality. For some sixty-five years he kept whatever records the company had on the backs of envelopes, so it is impossible to say how prosperous it became, but Trade gave away hundreds of thousands of dollars in philanthropy during his life and still managed to leave an estate of two or three million dollars when he died in 1913.

Trade and Mark are buried in the same cemetery but at different locations. Both their gravestones bear the Constantinian motto, *In hoc signo vinces*—"By this sign you shall conquer."

WILLIAM W. SMITH
1830 1913
IN HOC SIGNO VINCES
FATHER

BROTHER.
Andrew.
IN HOC SIGNO VINCES

Frank Winfield Woolworth

(1852–1919)

MERCHANT

Woodlawn Cemetery
Bronx, New York

When F. W. Woolworth fled from the life of a farm boy in upstate New York, he began his mercantile career working for nothing. It eventually paid off in nickels and dimes.

His first shop, "The Great Five Cent Store," flopped, but within a year he tried again, this time with prices all the way up to a dime. By the time he departed for that great big five-and-dime in the sky, there were over a thousand Woolworths here and in England. Thrift-conscious customers found everything from hairnets to frying pans and, in song and fact, boy met girl "in the five-and-ten-cent store."

Woolworth was exacting in business matters and often made unexpected visits to his stores, where, incognito, he shoplifted from the open counters to see if his managers were on their toes. But death, like the boss, has a way of arriving unexpectedly. When this exacting businessman died suddenly at his Long Island country home, he had neglected to sign a new will his lawyers had drawn up. The one-page will he had signed thirty years before left everything to his wife and appointed her sole executrix. Now his wife was mentally incompetent, suffering from premature senility, and his personal estate was estimated at forty million dollars. Had the court not appointed a guardian for her the previous year, had her two daughters and granddaughter (Barbara Hutton) not been independently wealthy, and had she not herself previously made a will leaving everything to them (including, now, everything of Woolworth's), which because of her incompetency could not be changed, the legal entanglements could have gone on for years.

As it was, the family did not have to dip into anybody else's cash register to build this mausoleum fit for a pharaoh. Its Egyptian motif was a popular trend in cemetery architecture during the twenties, and sometimes, today, boy meets girl by the sphinx.

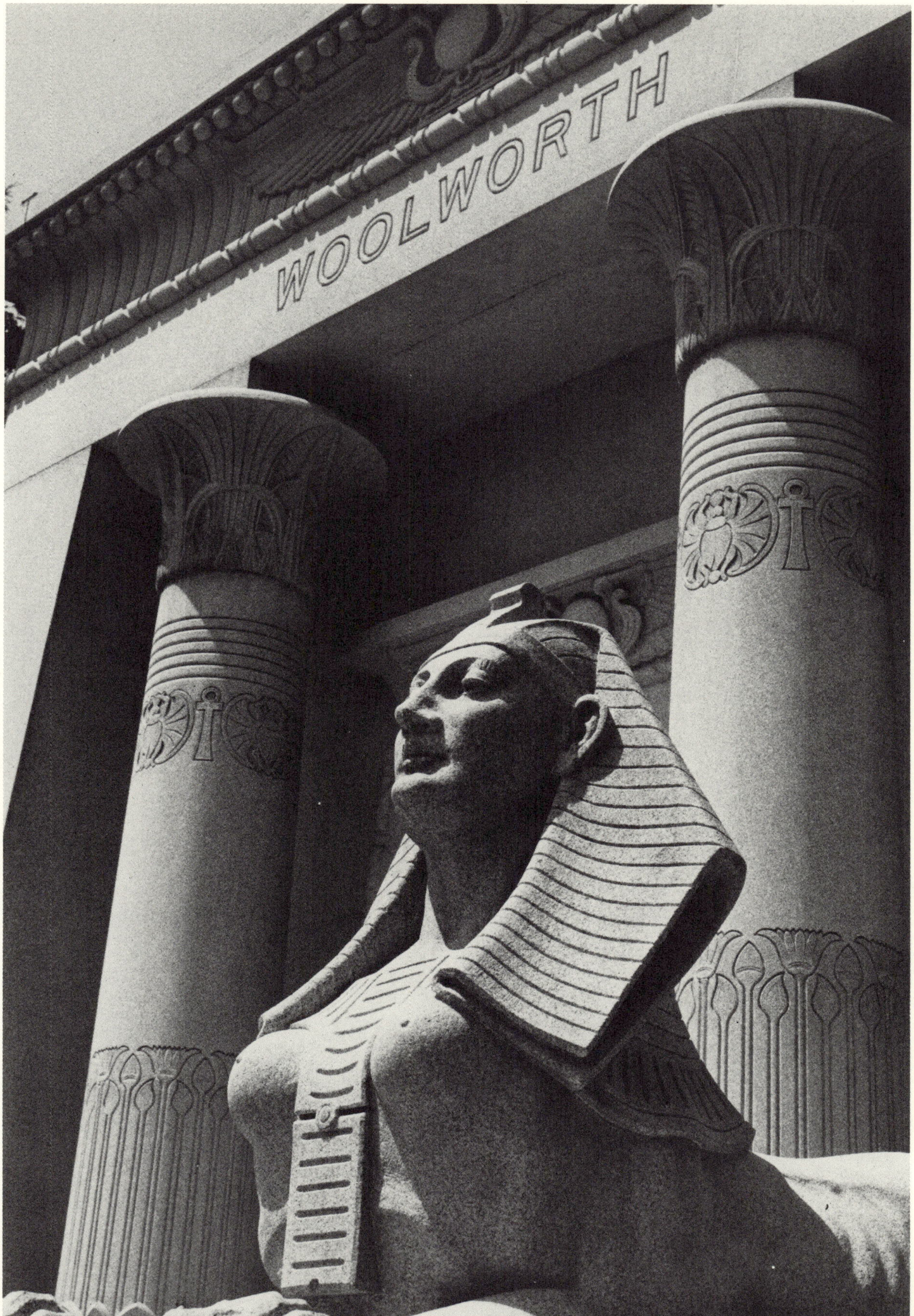
WOOLWORTH

Milton Snavely Hershey
(1857–1945)
CHOCOLATE MANUFACTURER

Hershey Cemetery
Hershey, Pennsylvania

If there was ever a "company town" in this nation of free enterprise, Hershey, Pennsylvania, is it. Still unincorporated and dominated by its major employer, Hershey is more like Disneyland than a factory town and affects street names such as Chocolate and Cocoa Avenues, chocolate-colored streetlights in the shape of chocolate kisses, pens with chocolate-colored ink, and cops in you-know-what-colored uniforms.

Milton Hershey built all this from scratch out of the lush countryside where he was born. Never having gotten beyond fourth grade, he lost his first job as a printer's devil in nearby Lancaster when his straw hat fell into the press one day and, casting around for new employment, took a position as an apprentice to a confectioner. After completing his apprenticeship he tried to make a go of it as a candymaker in Philadelphia, Denver, Chicago, and New York, without success. Back in Lancaster, he managed to build up a successful caramel business, but soon decided to switch to chocolate, because he wanted something that would retain the imprint of his name in the summer, which caramels wouldn't. Armed with a chocolate recipe of his own concoction, he sold his caramel business and bought twelve-hundred acres of land in the heart of the Pennsylvania Dutch dairy country, where he built a new factory and began mass-producing the five-cent candy bars that made him famous. Around the factory he constructed a complete town, all company owned, including shops, schools, churches, and homes that were rented to his employees.

Childless, Hershey and his wife raised four orphan boys and he gave away most of his millions during his lifetime to establish the Hershey Industrial School for orphans, now the Milton Hershey School. He remained active as chairman of the board of the company until the age of eighty-seven, and died the following year in Hershey Hospital after a heart attack. Eight orphan boys served as pallbearers and the entire clergy of his town—a Catholic priest and five Protestant ministers—officiated at the nondenominational service. His gleaming monument (no, it's white) dominates the entrance of the immaculately manicured cemetery overlooking the tidy town he created.

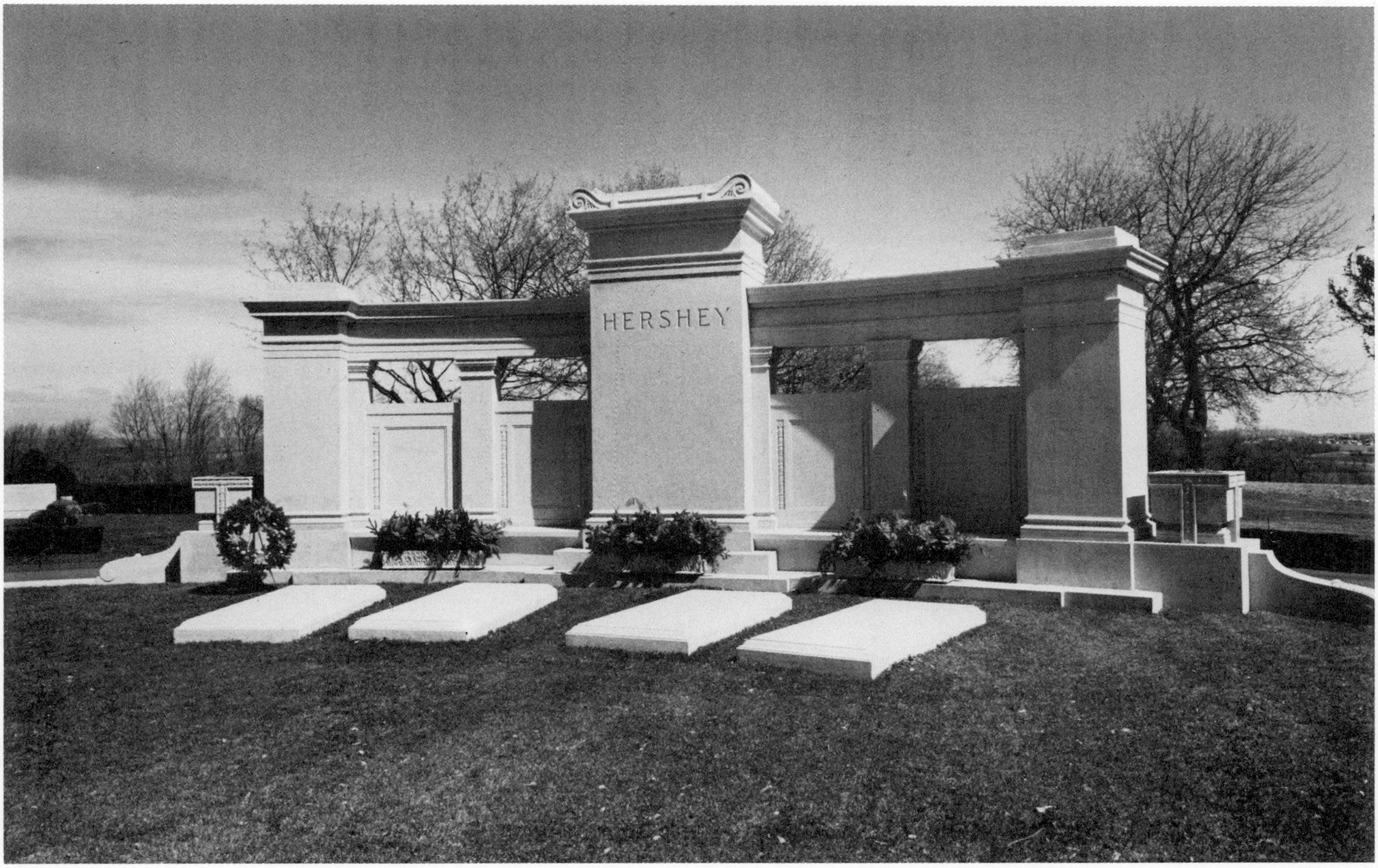
HERSHEY

You Can't Say One Without the Other

We do have our Tweedledees and Tweedledums. Ours were mortal, and they are forever consigned to joint appellation, although some were fierce individualists in life.

Meriwether Lewis
(1774–1809)

William Clark
(1770–1838)

EXPLORERS

Meriwether Lewis Park
Lewis County, Tennessee

Bellefontaine Cemetery
St. Louis, Missouri

If contemporary accounts are to be believed, Meriwether Lewis—formerly leader of the Lewis and Clark expedition and governor of the Louisiana Territory at the time of his death—put a gun to his head in the middle of the night at a trailside inn in the gloomy and savage Tennessee wilderness and creased his skull; cried out "O Lord!"; aimed again and hit his gut; crawled to the innkeeper's door and begged for help, which was refused; crawled back to his quarters and hacked aimlessly at himself with a sharp instrument; and finally managed to expire some hours later on the next day.

Lewis's money was not found on his body. Shortly thereafter the innkeeper, who had no known capital, moved to another town and bought a patch of the choicest land; his wife changed her already-inconsistent story several times; Lewis's half-breed servant, to whom he owed back wages, disappeared, and his watch turned up in New Orleans. The accepted verdict was "suicide"; but it seems incredible that this veteran soldier and frontiersman, experienced in weapons and combat, could have so thoroughly botched the job. He was buried where he fell, and his grave remained unmarked for forty years, until the Tennessee legislature appropriated five hundred dollars for the forlorn broken shaft that surmounts it today.

Meanwhile, his partner, William Clark, fared more respectably. Having been offered Lewis's governorship after his death, Clark tactfully declined but was later appointed governor of the Missouri Territory, fought nobly in the War of 1812, and became active in Indian affairs. He settled in St. Louis, where he died peacefully at the home of his eldest son (aptly named Meriwether Lewis Clark), and was buried with full honors. His grave, like Lewis's, was denied immediate recognition. Not until seventy years later was the imposing monument dedicated, endowed by his youngest son's will, topped by the larger-than-life bust overlooking the Mississippi, not far from where the famed expedition began.

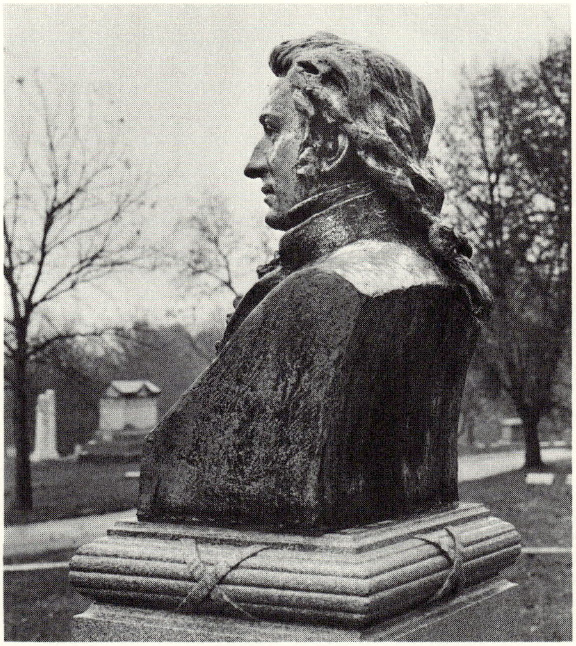

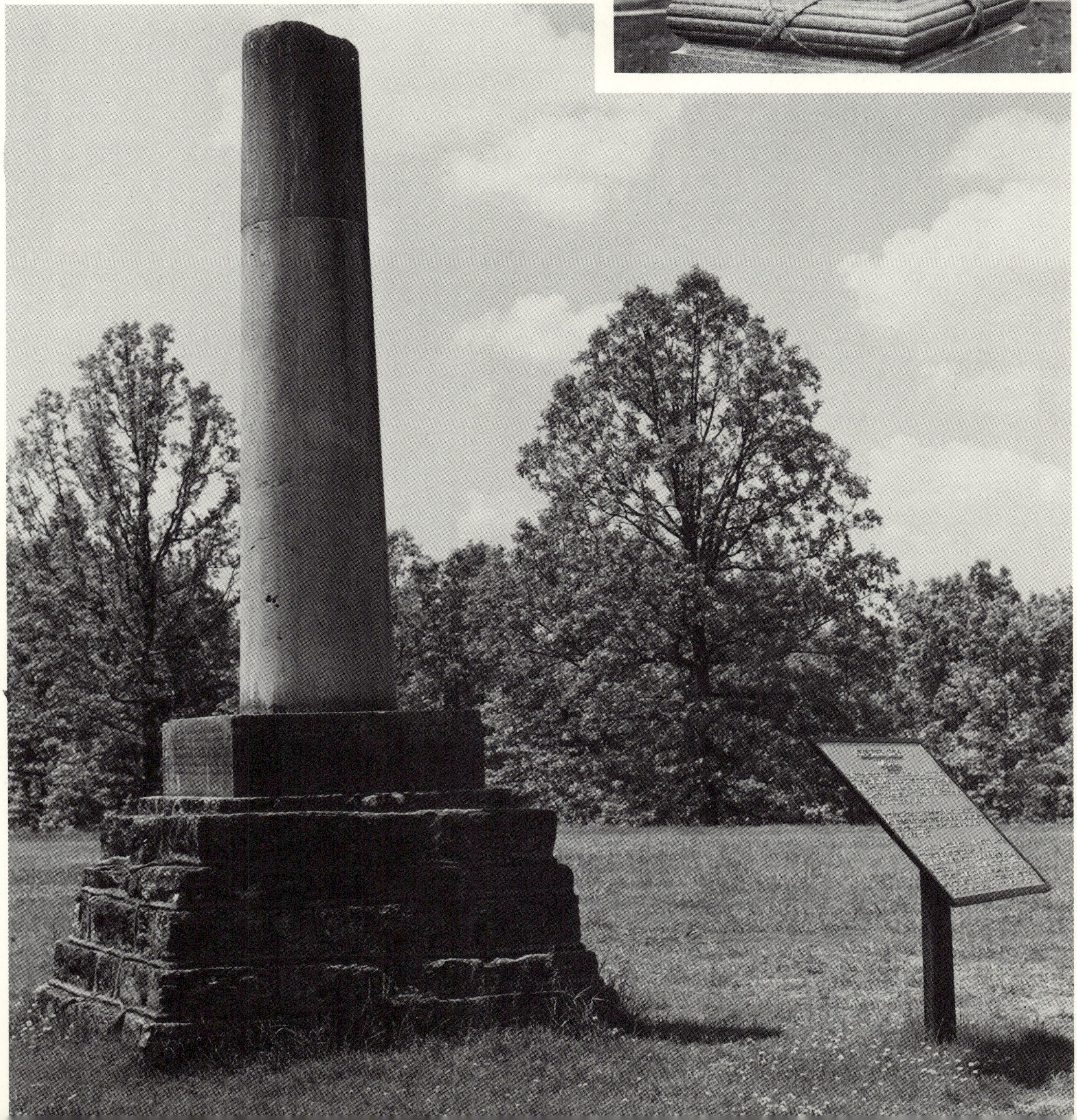

Henry Wells
(1805–1878)

William George Fargo
(1818–1881)

EXPRESSMEN

Oak Glen Cemetery
Aurora, New York

Forest Lawn Cemetery
Buffalo, New York

In its heyday the legendary Wells, Fargo & Company blanketed the American West, its extent bounded only by civilization. Its vermilion-and-gold Concord stages (custom-built in New Hampshire) carried passengers and freight everywhere, defended by ruthless messengers who gunned down thieves and highwaymen, hurling after the few who got away the grim promise that "Wells Fargo never forgets."

The names of Henry Wells and William Fargo are permanently enshrined in the lore of the frontier, but they were actually the founding fathers of a much more staid establishment back East: the American Express Company. Wells served as its first president for eighteen years, and Fargo succeeded him and held the post until his death. When gold was discovered in California, American Express, sniffing a sizable hunk of new business, decided to organize a western subsidiary, but Wells and Fargo scarcely resembled the macho subsidiary to which they lent their names. When they were not presiding over American Express, Wells was president of the local bank in his hometown of Aurora, New York, where he founded what is now Wells College; and Fargo, a leading citizen of Buffalo, got into the newspaper business and served two terms as mayor. Wells only went to California once on business, and complained that the trip made him "awful sore and tired." Fargo, so far as we can discover, never set foot west of Omaha.

Wells died of consumption, "the expressman's disease," at Glasgow, Scotland, where he was taken off a ship during a cruise intended to restore his failing health. Fargo succumbed three years later of a kidney ulceration, liver abcess, and pleurisy. Both rest quietly in the soil of New York State. But their names still ride our highways and streets to this day on armored trucks, latter-day Concord stages, painted in the same vermilion-and-gold colors as those that once rumbled across the prairies.

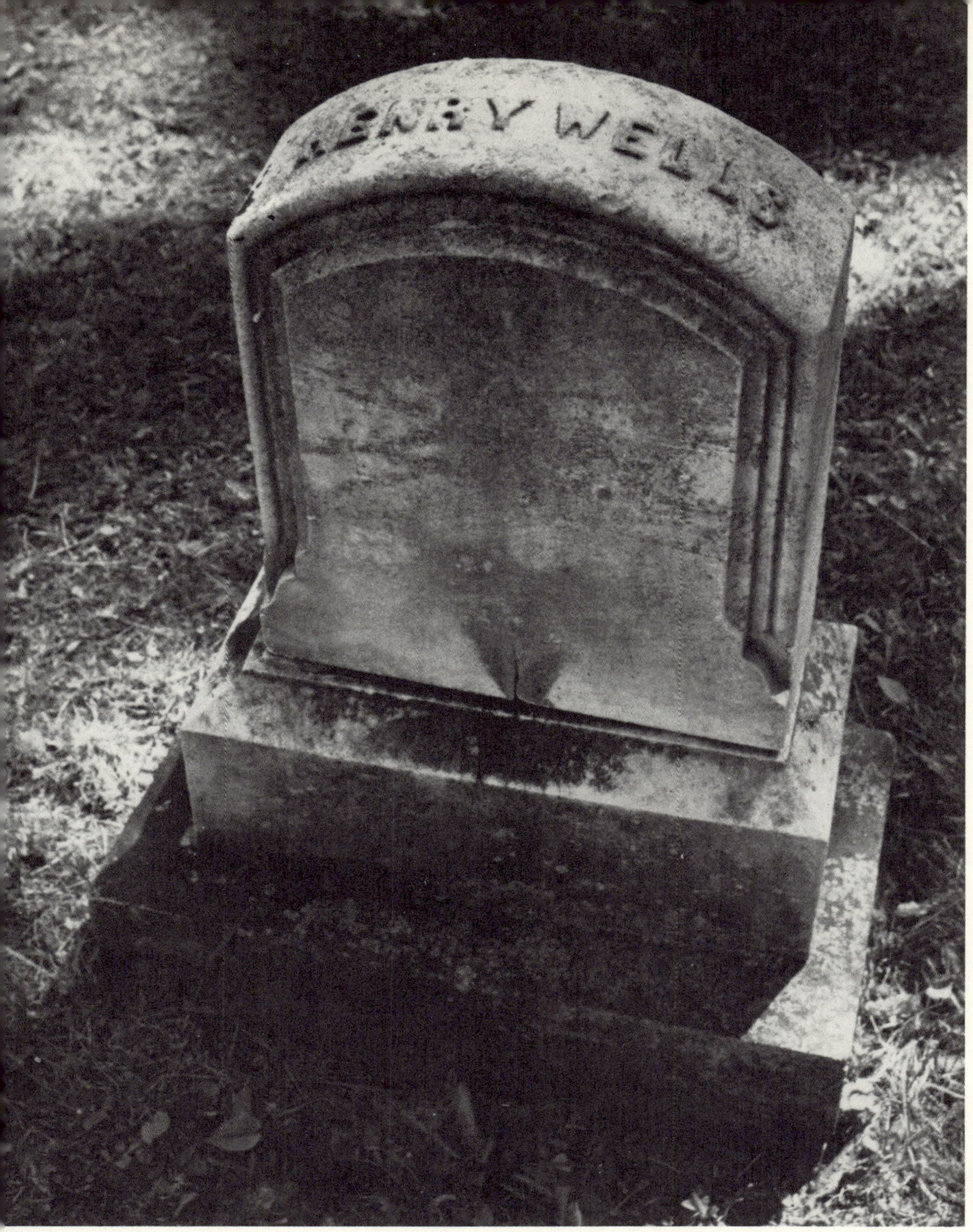
ENRY WELLS

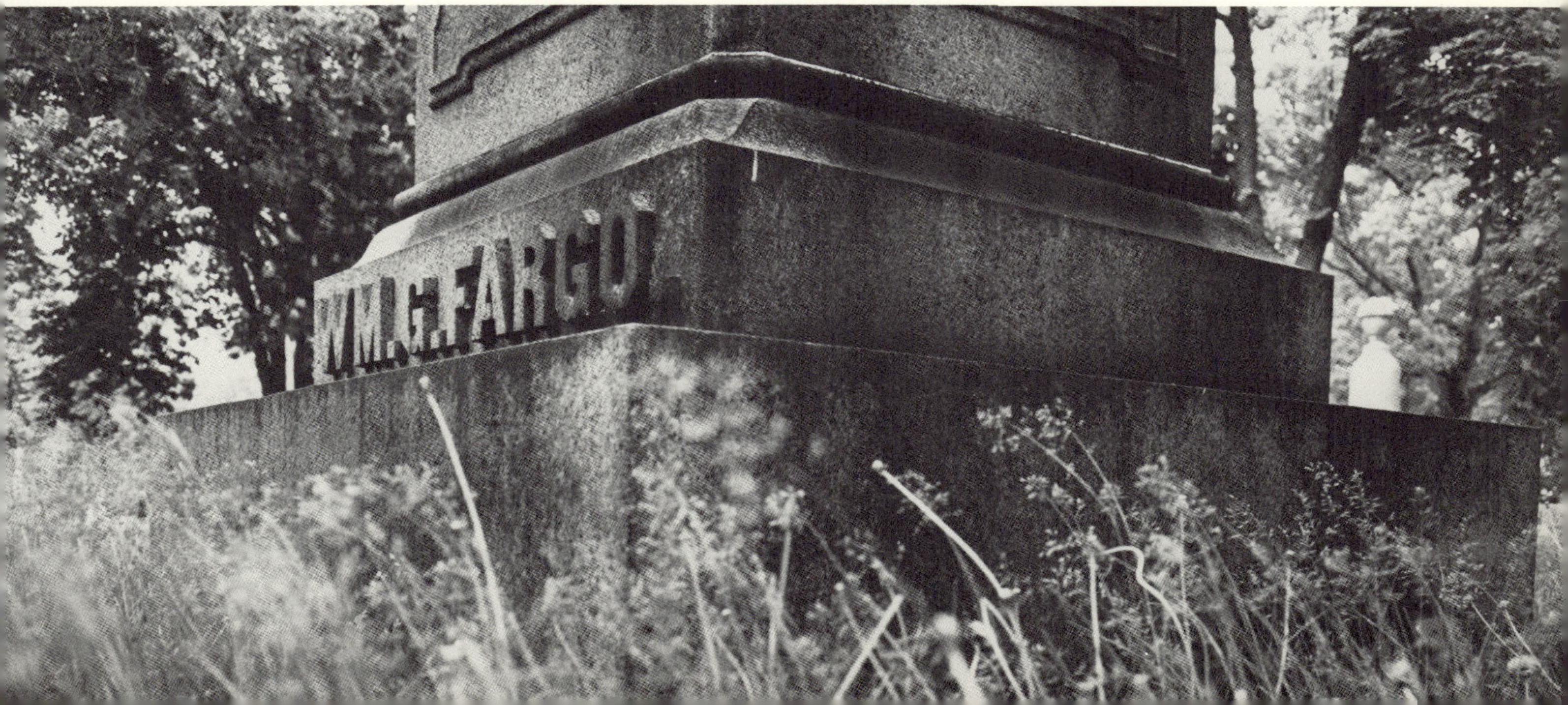
WM.G.FARGO

Chang and Eng Bunker

(1811–1874)

THE SIAMESE TWINS

Baptist Church Cemetery
White Plains, North Carolina

Chang and Eng Bunker excelled, perforce, at the art of accommodation. Their fraternal tie was a muscular band extending from below the chest down to and including a single navel. A pencil-thin line of liver tissue ran across the connecting strip. In their youth, although their normal stance was half-facing each other, the band was elastic and by stretching it they were able, as it were, to put their best feet forward.

Until they came of age, their proceeds from exhibition tours were garnered by a merchant, who probably had bought them from their mother in Siam. Once under the auspices of P. T. Barnum, they saved enough money to retire to a farm near Mount Airy, North Carolina, where they took the surname Bunker. At a time when group sex was not even a gleam in America's eye, they married sisters and between them fathered nineteen children. As time passed, the joint venture began to fray the sisters' nerves, and the couples set up separate households, each twin being master in his own. From then on, every three days without fail, Chang and Eng moved a mile and a half down the road from one house to the other.

The road in tandem was occasionally bumpy. Chang, more frail and volatile, liked the bottle, and although Eng did not share his hangovers he once found Chang's behavior discomfiting enough to ask if their local doctor could separate them, which he could not.

It is not surprising that Eng grumbled when, after leaving Chang's house on schedule one freezing January evening, he had to sit by the fire because Chang felt cold after the trip in an open wagon. The next night Chang complained of chills and chest pains, and at daybreak Eng awoke and found him dead. Terrified, he got the shakes, followed by a choking sensation and cramps. His family massaged and pulled his limbs, but within two hours he was dead also.

The doctors concluded that Chang had died from pneumonia and Eng from fright. Although Eng's part of the connecting band appeared fatty and well nourished, which Chang's did not, we now know that Eng's healthy condition could not have defended him against the infection from Chang's body. Endotoxins swarmed across the bridge of tissue into Eng's system. It was as if he had an abcess equal to his own size.

The Siamese twins were buried in the graveyard of a white clapboard country church in a double coffin under a double stone.

B
ENG BUNKER
MAY 11 1811
JAN 17 1874
HIS WIFE
SARAH A. YATES
DEC. 18 1822
APR. 29 1892
CHANG BUNKER
MAY 11 1811
JAN 17 1874
HIS WIFE
ADELAIDE YATES
OCT 11 1823
MAY 21 1917
SIAMESE TWINS CHANG AND ENG
BORN IN SIAM
BUNKER

Nathaniel Currier
(1813–1888)

James Merritt Ives
(1824–1895)
LITHOGRAPHERS

Green-Wood Cemetery
Brooklyn, New York

Currier's first resounding success was with a speedily produced print of a disastrous shipboard fire, complete with lurid details. Fires continued to be a big item after Ives, an aspiring artist who arrived as his bookkeeper and stayed as his partner, joined him. In an era before photojournalism, they served as the nation's eyes, and the long-and-short of it was that the lanky Currier and the roly-poly Ives had a keen sense of what would sell.

With precision and sentiment and lots of tomato-ketchup red, Currier and Ives recorded the essence of nineteenth-century America. Their "Cheap and Popular Pictures" brightened art-thirsty homespun living rooms with scenes of whaling adventures, syrupy domesticity, dangerous mountain passes on the westward trek, Indians, kittens, cartoons of pithy comment or stand-up social humor, even "The Bloomer Costume," which allowed the less daring a view of that outrageous garment. Shopkeepers posted the partners' current scenes as bulletins, changing them when something else made the news.

As the black-and-white lithographs came off the factory presses, a platoon of women sat around a table with the prototype in front of them, each painting in a different color, assembly-line fashion. The finished prints, costing from a quarter up to four dollars, overflowed bins in the retail store a few blocks away, where Horace Greeley often stopped to catch the latest news; and peddlers bought the smaller ones wholesale for six cents each and carried them in rucksacks out into the hinterlands.

Catering to the nation's zealous fascination with the final knell, Currier and Ives rolled out deathbed scenes of American notables as fast as they expired. Like most of their subjects, the partners died in their own homes: Currier from heart disease in New York City and Ives, seven years later, in suburban Rye.

Currier's funeral service, in the parlor of his house, ended with the hymn, "There Is a Green Hill Far Away." Over a nearer hill, in the same cemetery, lies Ives. Both are beneath rocks of ages, which stand in ponderous contrast to the airiness of their prints.

NATHANIEL CURRIER
BORN
MARCH 27, 1813

JAMES MERRITT IVES,
BORN MARCH 5, 1824.
DIED JANUARY 3, 1895

Charles Edward Merrill
(1885–1956)

Woodlawn Cemetery
West Palm Beach, Florida

Edmund Calvert Lynch
(1885–1938)

Druid Ridge Cemetery
Pikesville, Maryland

Edward Allen Pierce
(1874–1974)

Dean Hill Cemetery
Orrington, Maine

Charles Erasmus Fenner, II
(1876–1963)

Metairie Cemetery
New Orleans, Louisiana

Alpheus Crosby Beane
(1888–1937)

Magnolia Cemetery
Augusta, Georgia

STOCKBROKERS

Geese have their gaggle and beauties have their bevy but where, except in America, would stockbrokers have their thundering herd? The name Merrill Lynch, Pierce, Fenner & Beane (now Smith) goes together as naturally as ham and eggs but, ironically, these five men were never partners all at the same time. Two of them were already dead when the famous firm, which was to become the butt of jokes about "We the People" and lead to such advertising shenanigans as a herd of cattle charging out of a TV screen, was organized.

Charles Merrill made his first business coup at the age of thirteen, when he sold his newspaper route in Jacksonville's red-light district for seventy-five dollars. He eventually went to Wall Street, where he met Edmund Lynch, a Baltimore blue blood, one day at the YMCA. In 1914, they joined forces to form Merrill, Lynch & Co., but the comma was inadvertently dropped from a batch of the firm's letterheads and the name has been Merrill Lynch, without the comma, ever since.

After Lynch's death, Merrill merged with E. A. Pierce & Company, and, in 1941, with the firm of Fenner & Beane, to form what was to become the largest brokerage house in the world. Lynch's name was retained, perhaps out of respect for one of the original partners. Beane was also dead of a heart attack at the age of forty-eight, at the time of the combination, but in sound conservative style, it wasn't until 1957 that the firm got around to replacing his name with Smith's.

Merrill semiretired in 1944 and succumbed, twelve years later, of complications from a heart condition. Fenner remained active

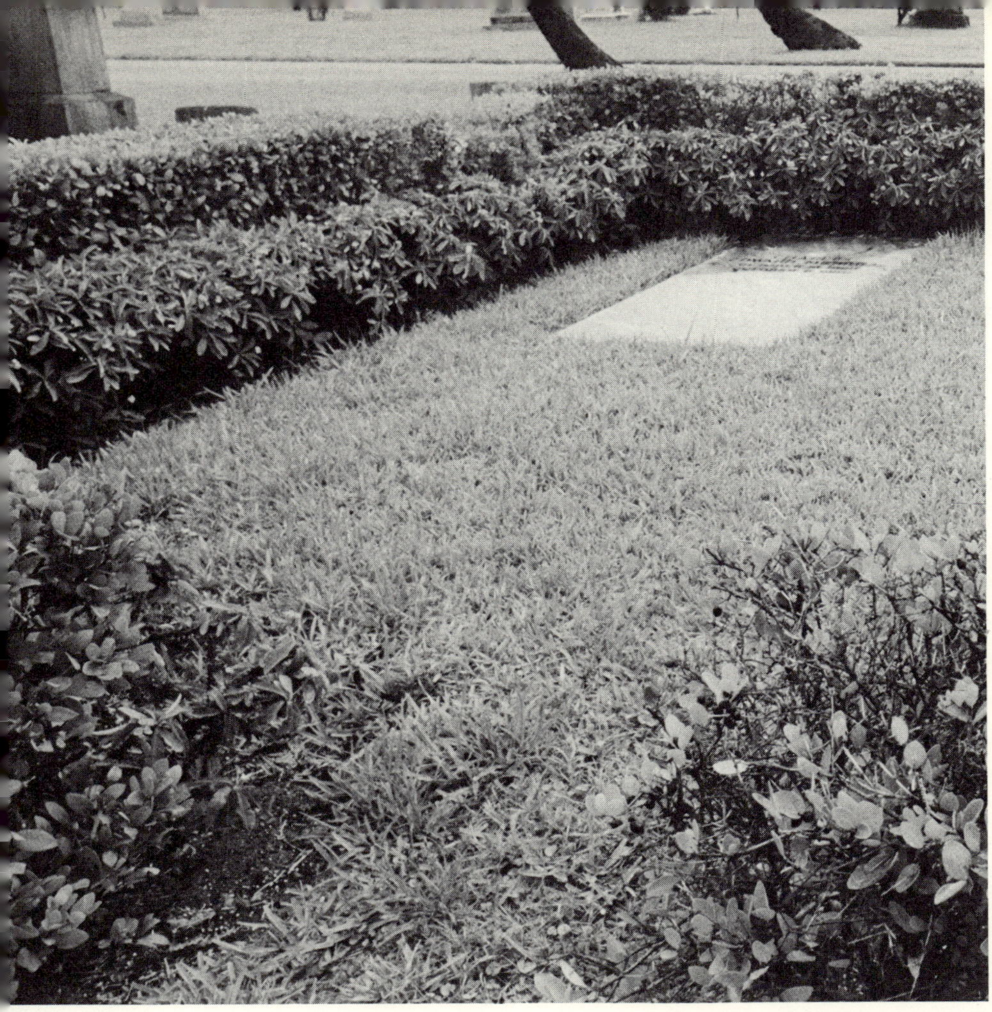

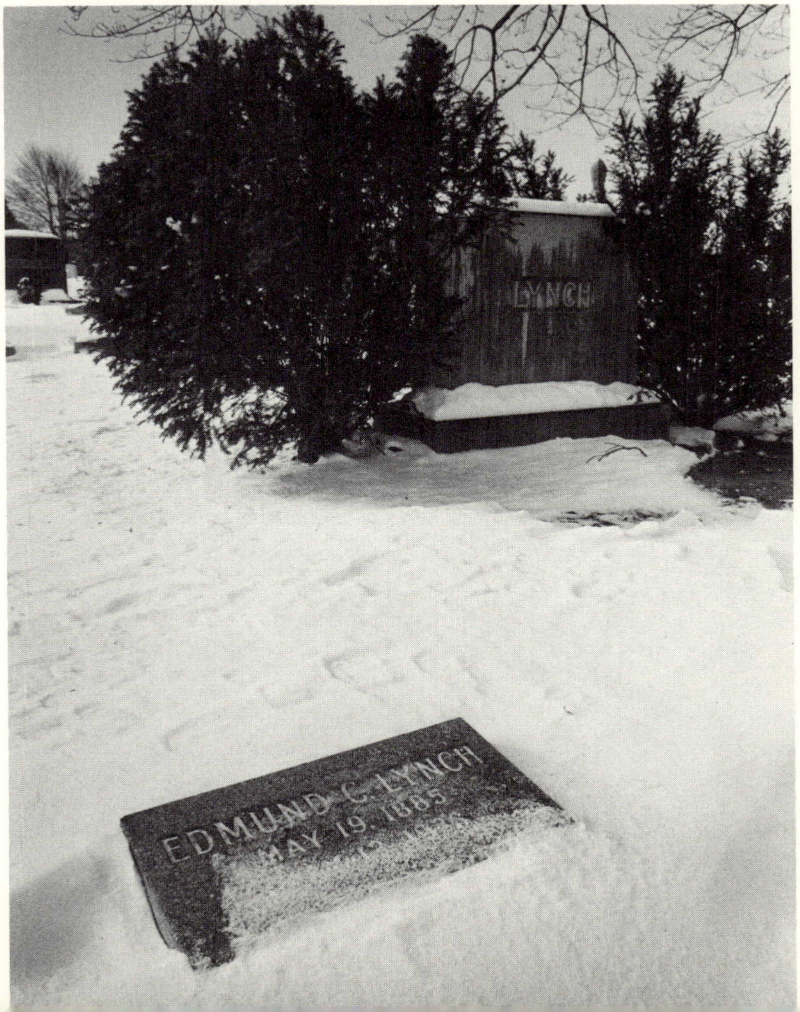
LYNCH
EDMUND C. LYNCH
MAY 19 1885

as a vice-president and voting stockholder until his death at his Louisiana country home, at the age of eighty-seven. But Pierce, a country boy from Maine, who had given up a hundred-dollar-a-week job in the lumber business to become a twenty-dollar-a-week clerk on Wall Street, was the granddaddy of them all; he died three months after celebrating his hundredth birthday.

The graves of these famous partners are scattered from the Gulf of Maine to the Gulf of Mexico, but they bump along together in the name that sounds, some say, like a beer barrel being rolled downstairs.

PIERCE
EDWARD A. PIERCE
1874 — 1974

BEANE

FENNER
VIRGINIA SCHRIEVER
WIFE OF CHARLES E. FENNER
CHARLES ERASMUS FENNER II
SEPTEMBER 4 1876—NOVEMBER 14 1963

Saints and Sinners

The law and the outlaw conjure visions of scrubby hills and horse chases. Most American swashbuckling and banditry took place in the Wild West. But the more sedate East also produced sinister characters.

Lola Montez
(1818–1861)
ADVENTURESS

Green-Wood Cemetery
Brooklyn, New York

Just how and when Marie Dolores Eliza Rosanna Gilbert of Limerick, Ireland, became Lola Montez of Spain is better left to historians. Lola may be the Spanish diminutive of Dolores, but there was nothing diminutive about this cookie. She had large flashing eyes, alabaster skin, a voluptuous body, and a temper that would shrivel stone. Before the age of thirty, she had shucked off the first of several husbands; taken numerous lovers, including Franz Liszt and Alexandre Dumas; and ensconced herself in the bedchamber of the King of Bavaria, then sixtyish, who called her Lolita, and whom she infected with syphillis, which eventually killed them both. She so completely dominated him that he made her a countess, and wags referred to his puppet government as the Lolaministerium. Within a few years, public resentment against her became so great that the king, realizing that he had been used, was forced to expel her and to abdicate.

Lola fancied herself a dancer and, after being deposed from the throne of Bavaria, she danced her way to America, where her famous and, at least for those days, erotic Spider Dance took the country by storm. She drew large audiences and people would pay a dollar to shake her hand and gape at a countess who smoked cigars, carried a pistol, and kicked, screamed, and clawed if anyone crossed her. The riding crop was her second most effective weapon. Judging from the number of affairs she is known to have had, she must have been the greatest lover of her generation. But underlying everything she said and did was her cynical contempt for men; she humiliated them in public, assaulted and battered them, lashed them with her tongue, threatened to kill them, drove them to suicide, and it might perhaps be more accurate to characterize her as her generation's greatest ballbreaker.

After a stormy tour of Australia, Lola returned to New York. Her stage talent, if she ever had any, was on the wane and the spirochetes were taking their inexorable toll. She became pale and haggard, her famous eyes were now sunken, and her body was literally wasting away. She lived alone in cheap rooming houses and spent the last years of her life visiting local asylums, preaching to prostitutes about the dangers of venereal disease, which some writers have regarded as her penance. Toward the end, she was afflicted with paralytic seizures, loss of speech, drooling at the mouth, and incontinence. The press, which had a field day with her life, ignored her death, but when this photograph was taken, a hundred-and-sixteen years later, her grave had just been freshly seeded.

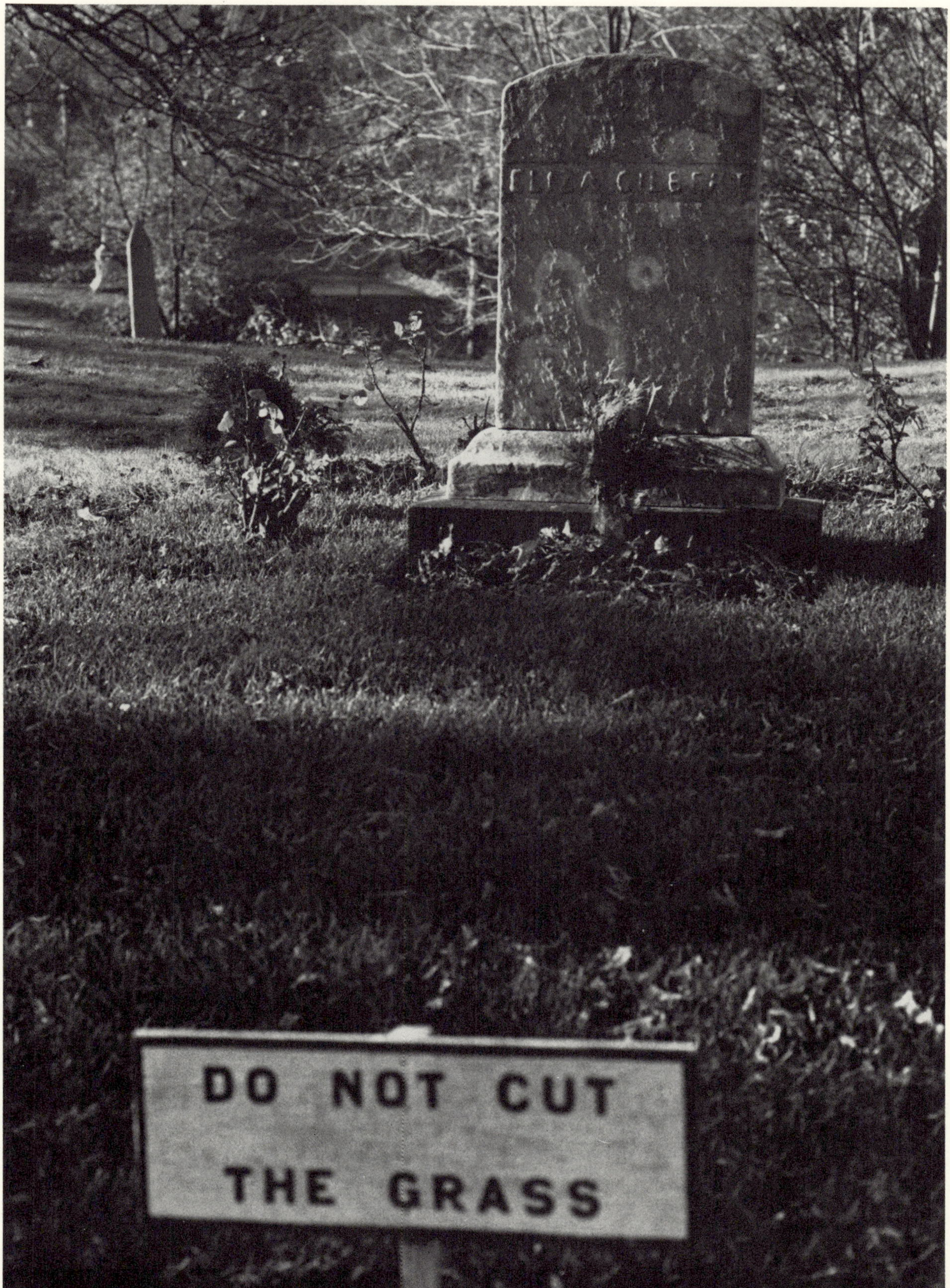
DO NOT CUT
THE GRASS

James Butler (Wild Bill) Hickok
(1837–1876)

Martha Jane Cannary (Calamity Jane) Burke
(1852?–1903)

FRONTIER CHARACTERS

*Mount Moriah Cemetery
Deadwood, South Dakota*

The sleepy burg of Deadwood, Dakota Territory, woke up pronto when Wild Bill Hickok and Calamity Jane rode into town, decked out in new clothes, shouting huzzas and firing pistols in the air. These two Frankie-and-Johnnys ended up buried together, which we think is sufficient license to put them together again in these pages.

Wild Bill was nominally on the side of law and order, although his eligibility for canonization may reasonably be disputed. During his career as a stagecoach driver, Union spy, and deputy marshal in some of the roughest towns in Kansas, he earned the nickname of Prince of Pistoleers and a bloody reputation as the fastest and deadliest gunslinger in the West. Estimates of the number of men he killed range from a paltry seven to more than a hundred, but he always boasted that he never killed unless in the line of duty or in absolute self-defense. After a brief stint with Buffalo Bill's Wild West Show, he settled down to a gambling life in Deadwood, a life abruptly terminated by a shot in the back of the head during a poker game, when he broke his own rule never to sit with his back to the door. The hand he held was two pairs of aces and eights, since that day to become known as the Dead Man's Hand.

Calamity Jane was, to put it charitably, a camp follower and a man's woman. She drank and cussed her way across the frontier, dressed in men's clothing, tagging along with military and surveying expeditions, and eventually settling in Deadwood, where she took up with Wild Bill. After his murder, she tramped aimlessly from bar to brothel, hiring out occasionally as an ox-team driver. Shortly before her death, she turned up again in Deadwood, where she allowed herself to be photographed leaning blearily against the fence enclosing Wild Bill's grave. By then a hopeless alcoholic, she took an ill turn and died of "inflammation of the bowels," just one day before the twenty-seventh anniversary of Bill's death.

Her last words may not have been "Bury me next to Bill," but that's exactly what happened. The white marker in the foreground of the picture is a replica of one erected by Hickok's friend, "Colorado Charlie" Utter. The stones in the background are of recent vintage, embedded in boulders and concrete to discourage souvenir hunters.

TO PREACHER SMITH GRAVE
CALAMITY JANE
WILD BILL
JACK McCALL
— in —
DEADWOOD
August 2nd 1876
Pard we will
meet again
in the happy
Hunting ground
to part no more.
GOOD BYE
COLORADO
CHARLIE.
C.H.UTTER.

William Barclay (Bat) Masterson
(1853–1921)
FRONTIER PEACE OFFICER

*Woodlawn Cemetery
Bronx, New York*

Does Bat Masterson, the last of the old-time gunfighters, lie with a bullet in his spleen and a sneer on his face in some forgotten, windswept, tumbleweed burying ground in Deadwood or Tombstone? No, he does not. Sad to record, the bones of the erstwhile sheriff of Dodge City lie in middle-class respectability in the Bronx.

Railroad builder, buffalo hunter, Indian fighter, frontier scout, gold prospector, deputy marshal, sheriff, gambler, gunslinger: Bat Masterson could legitimately claim all these occupations on his résumé, and his early achievements are forever enshrined in the lore of the American West. He ranked with such frontier peace officers as Wyatt Earp and Wild Bill Hickok, who "shot their way to heaven" in the cause of justice and on the side of law and order.

What is not so well known is that at the age of forty-eight Bat hung up his guns, moved to New York City, and became a newspaper man, spending the rest of his life covering sports events, particularly boxing, which was his special interest, and eventually becoming sports editor of the *Morning Telegraph*. He died suddenly, while working at his desk.

MASTERSON
WILLIAM BARCLAY MASTERSON
1854 — 1921
LOVED BY EVERYONE

Lizzie Andrew Borden

(1860–1927)
ALLEGED MURDERESS

Oak Grove Cemetery
Fall River, Massachusetts

> Lizzie Borden took an axe
> And gave her mother forty whacks;
> And when that job was nicely done,
> She gave her father forty-one.

Everybody thinks of Lizzie Borden as one of the brightest threads in our national fabric of cutthroats. Not everybody knows that Lizzie was, in fact, acquitted of the hideous crime described in the jump-rope jingle we learned as children.

It was common knowledge in Victorian Fall River that no excess love was shared among Lizzie, her father Andrew Jackson Borden, a prominent businessman, and his second wife Abby Durfee Borden, whom he had married when Lizzie was only four years old. No one knows how deeply these resentments smouldered in the twenty-eight years that intervened before the eruption that terminated the marital relationship. Nevertheless, one hot August morning in 1892, Mr. and Mrs. Borden were found acutely disengaged from life by reason of savage axe wounds about the head. They were buried in a decapitated state, and Lizzie was indicted and brought to trial. The sensation of the double murder was heightened when both heads were produced as exhibits, causing Lizzie to slump down in a dead faint.

After her acquittal, when the prosecution failed to prove its case beyond a reasonable doubt, Lizzie moved to another house nearby. She remained in Fall River the rest of her life, ostracized by the community, which didn't give a dang what the jury found, and living largely as a recluse. She traveled occasionally and must have lived comfortably, since she left a substantial estate. Christened Lizzie Andrew, in later years she affected Lizbeth Andrews, as her name appears on the family monument. When she entered a hospital in 1926 for an operation, she registered as Mary Smith Borden, and out of kindness the staff pretended not to recognize her. When she died, she was buried secretly at night, and friends attending the funeral service the next day were told the burial had already taken place.

The graves are laid out in a curious triangular arrangement said to have been planned by Lizzie herself: Andrew and Abby form the base of the triangle and Lizzie the apex—or the feet and the head. One wonders if the arrangement silently conveys some macabre pun. To this day, fresh flowers are occasionally found by Lizzie's stone; placed by whom, or why, no one seems to know.

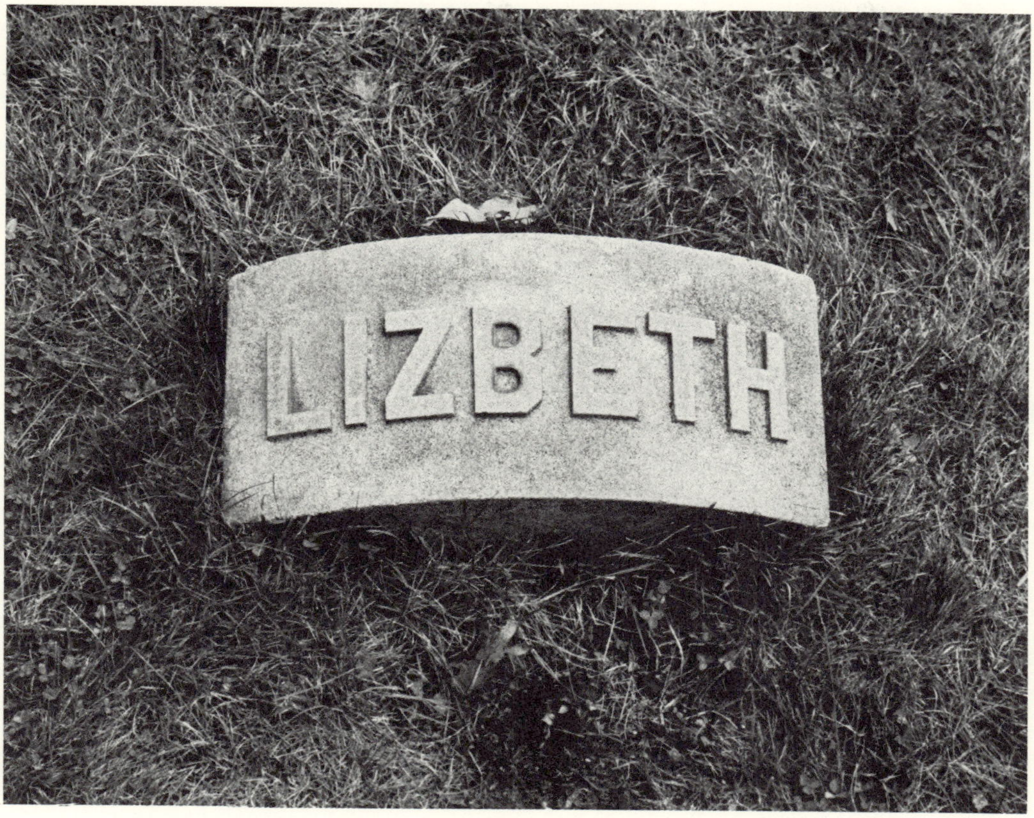
LIZBETH

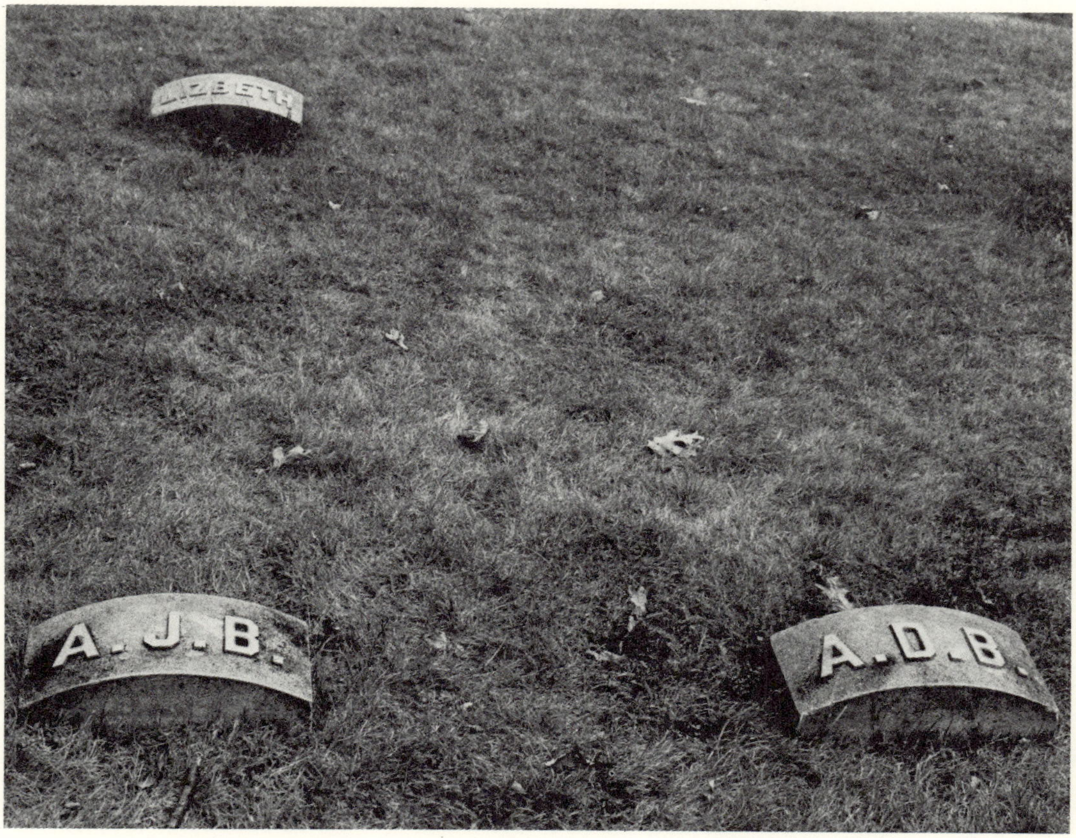
LIZBETH
A. J. B.
A. D. B.

Winners

Another kind of daring brings fortunes to many Americans. Once achieved, success may manifest itself through the traditional virtue of frugality or the equally traditional trait of showmanship. The Big Skinflint takes her place among the Big Spenders.

James Fisk, Jr.
(1834–1872)
FINANCIAL BUCCANEER

Prospect Hill Cemetery
Brattleboro, Vermont

"Jubilee Jim" Fisk's flamboyant path to the grave began in a gaily painted peddler's cart in Vermont and ended in New York City in a rosewood coffin with gold handles. He made the mistake of introducing his paramour, actress Josie Mansfield, to his business colleague, the handsome and debt-ridden Edward S. Stokes. A greedy triangular feud over love and money finally erupted when Stokes shot Fisk twice as he climbed the steps of the Grand Central Hotel.

Mortally wounded but still on his feet, Fisk was helped to a hotel room where eight doctors poked and prodded his stomach, trying to retrieve the fatal bullet. His diamonds were removed from his expansive shirtfront for safekeeping. His lawyer prevailed upon Fisk to make his last will and testament; one of the subscribing witnesses was his equally infamous partner, Jay Gould.

The following morning, Jubilee Jim slipped peacefully from a coma into death, thus providing the *New York Times* with the opportunity to point out that, in his unconscious state, Fisk "was spared the pain of looking back upon his past, or of contemplating his future."

Although Fisk's financial shenanigans hurt many innocent investors, his reputation as a lively, effervescent scamp brought out the crowds for his funeral, unmatched since Lincoln's. His Erie Railroad stockholders were more relieved than sorry. But members of New York's Ninth Regiment, which Fisk had saved from financial ruin, wept as their colonel, resplendent in a two-thousand-dollar white uniform, lay in state in the Opera House that he had erected with Erie money. Later, the regiment, three-hundred-and-fifty strong, marched to muffled drums to the funeral train that would carry him home.

The train was draped in black crepe and throngs turned out to salute it en route. At Brattleboro, farmers swarmed in from the countryside for a last look. After prayers of a length appropriate to the precarious state of the deceased's soul, Jubilee Jim was buried in a first-class spot on a bluff overlooking the Connecticut River. The show was over. Brattleboro citizens raised the money for his inimitable marble monument, the lovelies at the four corners representing his chief enthusiasms: steamships, railroads, stocks, the theater—and, of course, women.

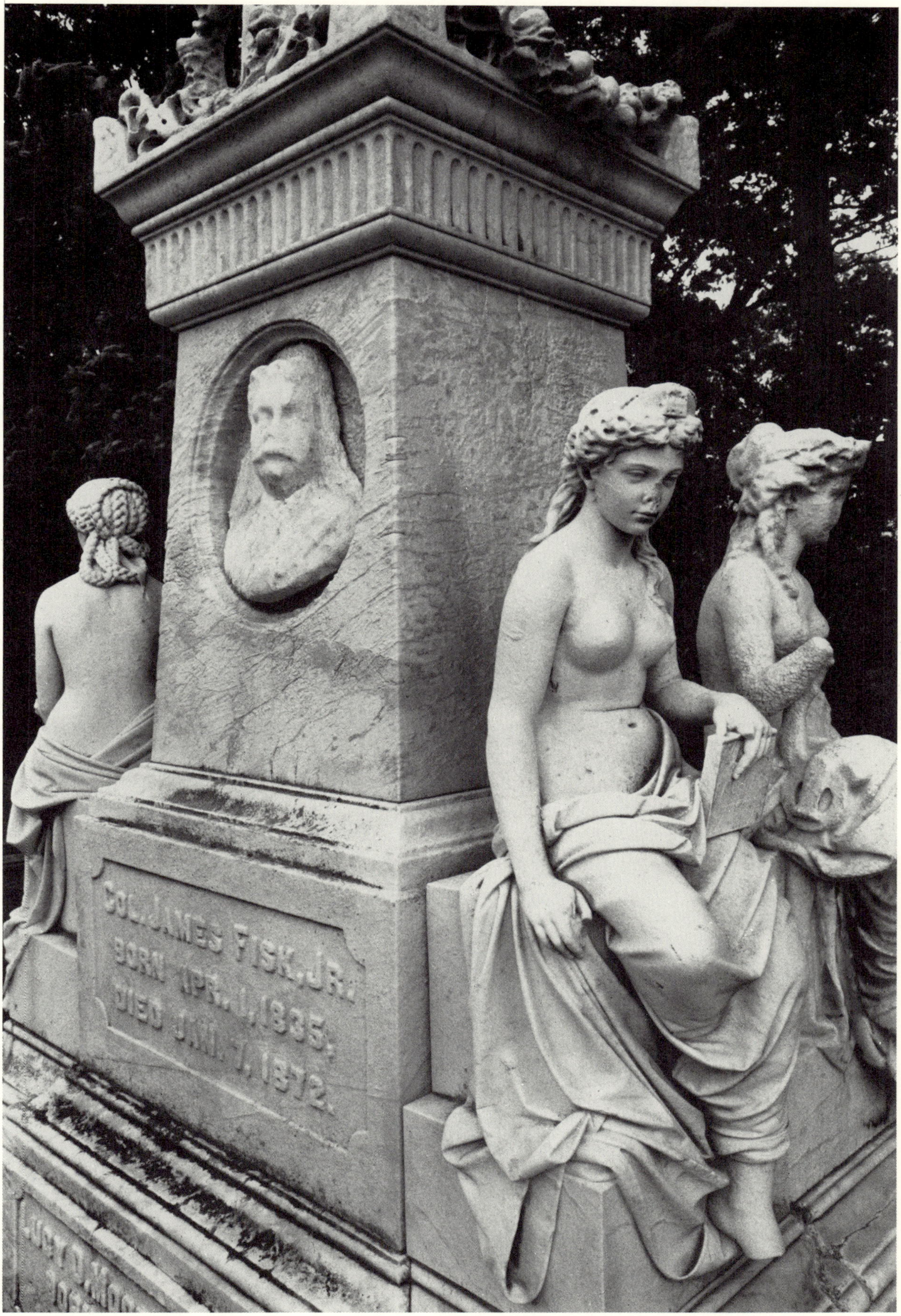
COL. JAMES FISK, JR.
BORN APR. 1, 1835;
DIED JAN. 7, 1872.

EDWARD HENRY GREEN
BORN
FEB. 6, 1821
OBT.
MAR. 19, 1902
HETTY H. R. GREEN
HIS WIFE
BORN
NOV. 21, 1834
OBT.
JULY 3, 1916

Henrietta Howland Robinson (Hetty) Green
(1835–1916)

FINANCIER

Immanuel Church Cemetery
Bellows Falls, Vermont

Publicly she was hailed as the world's greatest financier. Privately she was dubbed the "Witch of Wall Street." Hetty Green was shrewd in money matters and reprehensibly cheap. Inheriting a comfortable six million, she wheeled-and-dealed it into a fortune estimated between one hundred and two hundred million. She looked like the rag-and-bone lady as she directed her interests—railroads, real estate, moneylending—from a courtesy desk made available to her by a Wall Street bank. On unpredictable mornings she tortured bank clerks and vice-presidents alike by admonishing them to be sure the money in her checking account—often up to thirty million dollars—was available, as she "might just need it" later in the day.

Hetty did not pay taxes, nor did she submit to charitable appeals. No one could be sure where she legally lived. To escape legal confrontations she would flit from a cold-water flat in Hoboken, to a cheap boardinghouse in Brooklyn, to a hovel in downtown Manhattan, never putting her name on the door. For many years she dragged her daughter, who served as cleaning woman and cook on a miserly budget, with her. A regular feature on the Green menu was oatmeal, which Hetty claimed gave her strength to fight "those Wall Street wolves."

She mistrusted lawyers (although she was constantly involved in litigation) and doctors. The latter mistrust was probably responsible, through neglect, for the amputation of her son's gangrenous right leg, which was interred in the family plot and, upon his death forty-seven years later, skillfully reunited with the rest of him. Her partiality toward free clinics incensed the doctors, who recognized her in the long waiting lines.

As her eightieth birthday approached, the richest woman in the world heard of a private physician who charged fifty cents for an office visit. Her pain was sufficiently acute to force Hetty into the examination room. There it was revealed that she had an enormous hernia, and that she was using a stick, held up by her leg and underclothes, to support the protuberance. But the proposed surgical fee of one-hundred-fifty dollars was unthinkable. She stomped out, hernia, stick, and all.

A series of paralyzing strokes finally trapped the intrepid Hetty Green, and within weeks she was dead. The *Boston Evening Transcript* headlined the event: SHE, TOO, LEFT HERS BEHIND. Her body was transported from New York City to Bellows Falls, where she joined her husband, a gentle man whom she had seldom seen, in his family's plot.

John Pierpont Morgan

(1837–1913)

BANKER

Cedar Hill Cemetery
Hartford, Connecticut

When John D. Rockefeller paid tribute to J. Pierpont Morgan's boldness in dealing with the financial crisis of 1907, he added, with priceless understatement, "And he is not a rich man, either."

Hetty Green was richer and Jubilee Jim Fisk and Diamond Jim Brady were more flamboyant, but Pierpont Morgan had one thing over them: class. The characteristics that impelled him into the unquestioned position of the foremost banking figure in the world were his personal integrity and his unflagging reliance on the "gentlemen's agreement," a phrase he himself coined. A few months before his death, he was asked by a hostile House committee investigating the "Money Trust":

Q. Is not commercial credit based primarily upon money or property?
A. No sir, the first thing is character.
Q. Before money or property?
A. Before money or property or anything else. Money cannot buy it.... Because a man I do not trust could not get money from me on all the bonds in Christendom.

Shortly after the hearings, from which Morgan emerged largely unscathed, he set sail for Egypt to regain the strength sapped by his advancing years and the strain of testifying under fire. His condition worsened, and he was taken to Rome and set up in a hotel apartment under the care of the finest Italian physicians. Fresh butter and eggs were rushed to him from his farm in New York. But he was not able to retain nourishment, and at the end one of the most prominent symbols of wealth we have ever seen died, quite literally, of starvation.

Morgan's body was embalmed, brought back to New York for a magnificent funeral, and buried in the family mausoleum in Hartford. That pinkish-red colossus is reminiscent both of the monolithic House of Morgan at 23 Wall Street, completed after his death, and the mortarless Pierpont Morgan Library, which he built next to his home at the corner of Madison Avenue and Thirty-Sixth Street to house his vast collection of manuscripts and rare books. Both still stand today, and J. P. Morgan might be said to have three mausoleums instead of the one ordinarily enjoyed by the wealthy departed.

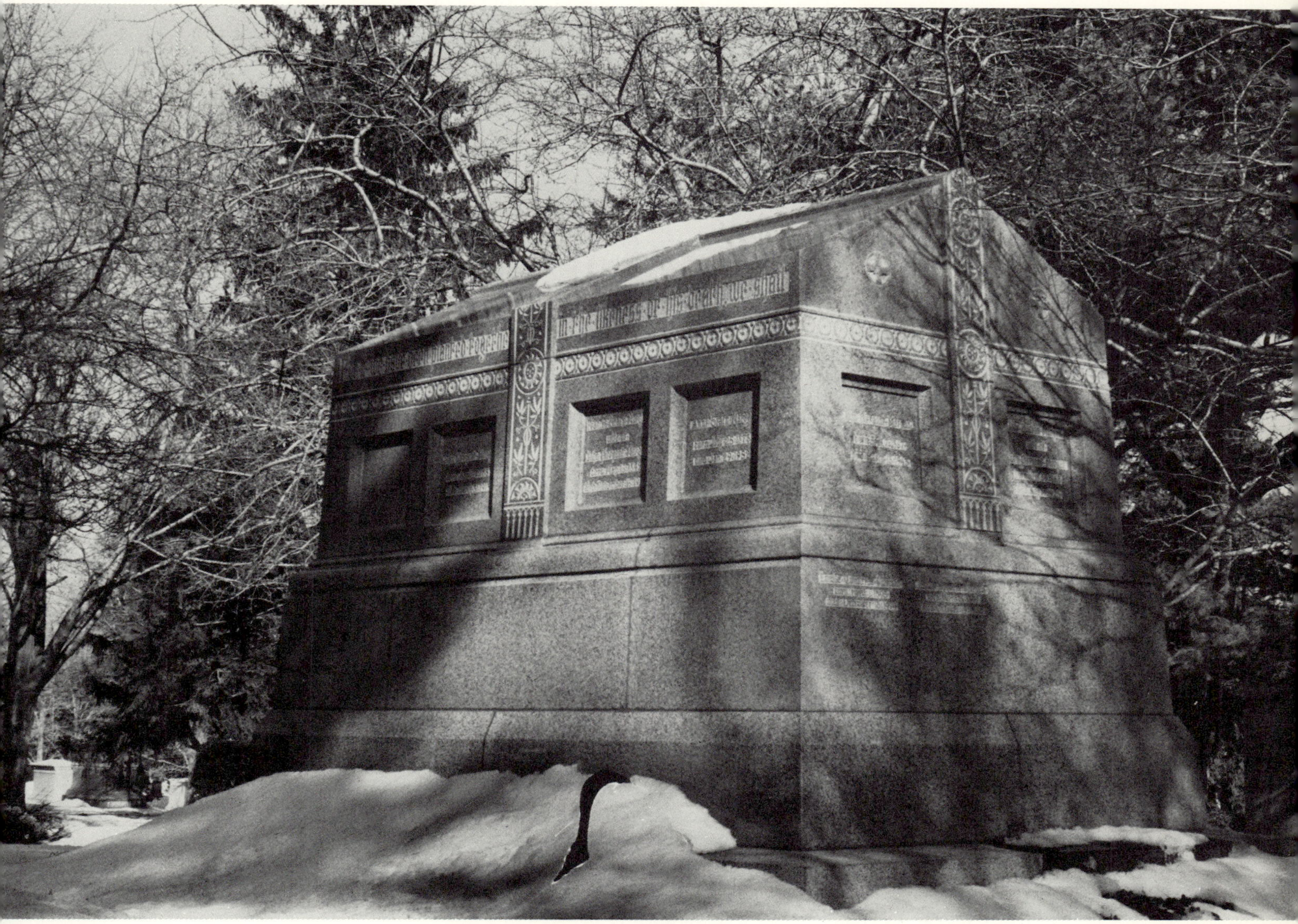

James Buchanan (Diamond Jim) Brady
(1856–1917)
SALESMAN

Holy Cross Cemetery
Brooklyn, New York

Diamond Jim Brady never drank liquor but frequently suffered from acute indigestion. At the height of his gastronomical prowess, Diamond Jim thought nothing of tossing down six dozen oysters as a snack. His stomach, which doctors found to be six times larger than normal, billowed out to touch the table as he wallowed his way through twelve-course meals. Advised to diet and exercise, Brady ignored the former and dabbled in the latter on a gold-plated bicycle, with diamonds on the handlebars to give "a touch of class."

He wasn't called Diamond Jim for nothing. In order to give "a touch of class" to himself, Brady began sporting diamonds when he began his career as a railroad-equipment salesman. Before long he was sparkling from stem to stern; even his underwear buttons and garter clasps were gems. He gave laundry-basket-size presents of food to his friends at Christmas, bought a gold Tiffany chamber pot for Lillian Russell, and was always a soft touch for a loan. Facing a kidney operation and convinced he was going to die, Brady tore up dozens of IOUs. (After the operation, which was successful, he provided funds for a urological clinic to show his gratitude.) When his mistress jilted him, he said, "There ain't a woman in the world who'd marry an ugly looking guy like me." Not one to remain despondent, he took lessons in the one-step and the grizzly-bear from Vernon and Irene Castle, and then went out on the town to lumber around the dance floor all night, bringing along a spare partner for when the first one wore out.

In December 1916, suffering from diabetes and heart and kidney ailments, he went to Atlantic City to meet "the man in the white nightgown." There he set up housekeeping in a thousand-dollar-a-week hotel suite with a glass-enclosed veranda, where he could watch the Boardwalk crowds. One of his last acts was to buy a six-thousand-four-hundred-dollar pair of glasses, set with rose diamonds, as a present for his dog. One April morning his valet tried to awaken him, but the sweet-tempered Brady had died of a heart attack.

Diamond Jim's will left his thirty sets of sparklers, which were valued at one million dollars, to assorted friends. But the big spender himself ended up in the backwaters of Brooklyn. If a gravestone represents an entrance to the Heavenly Hotel, it looks as if Diamond Jim isn't in as much of a pleasure palace as he would have liked.

B
IN MEMORY
JOHN BRADY
MARY A. BRADY-LUCAS
JAMES B. BRADY
SON OF JOHN AND MARY A. BRADY
DANIEL M. BRADY
HARRIET BRADY MATHIEU
BRADY

Losers

While some succeed grandly, others must fail grandly. These people are losers. Some have been simply overlooked in the shuffle. Others endear themselves to us by a comic, larger-than-life, American bumbling.

GEORGE W.
WHISTLER
Born
in Indiana
May 19. 1800.
Died
April 7. 1849.

George Washington Whistler

(1800–1849)

WHISTLER'S FATHER

Evergreen Cemetery
Stonington, Connecticut

James Abbott McNeill Whistler once wrote a letter to his father about his artistic aspirations. His mother answered it: "It is quite natural you should think . . . you should prefer the profession of an Artist, your father did so before you. I have often congratulated myself his talents were more usefully applied."

When Major George Washington Whistler left military service, it was not for the life of an artist. He was a civil engineer, and in 1842 he went to Russia to supervise the construction of the Czar's railroad between Moscow and St. Petersburg. His heart weakened by a cholera attack, he died there, and his body was shipped back to America.

Whistler's mother hangs in the Louvre. Whistler's father lies in an unkempt corner of a cemetery near the Connecticut shore. Here, but not in the Louvre, you can hear the whistles of trains in the night.

John Augustus Sutter
(1803–1880)
CALIFORNIA PIONEER

Moravian Cemetery
Lititz, Pennsylvania

One of the ironies of our national history is that John Sutter, who is sometimes called the Father of California, and whose name is practically synonymous with the gold rush, died back east, stone broke.

Sutter arrived in California, then a Mexican province, on July 3, 1839. Within a few years he had become a Mexican citizen and received land grants totaling about two-hundred-and-twenty-nine square miles, which he built up into a thriving estate, with several thousand horses and cattle. His property did not suffer from its location on the main overland trail routes. The future continued to look bright when, after the Mexican War, California became a part of the United States, and the munificent landowner went as a delegate to the state constitutional convention.

Meanwhile, in January 1848, one of his crews, blasting away some rock to deepen the channel of a millrace, set off a charge and blew smack into the Mother Lode. It was the beginning of Sutter's ruin. When word trickled out that gold had been discovered at Sutter's Mill, it touched off the onslaught of the forty-niners. His lands were overrun with squatters, his cattle were killed, and his workmen deserted. In 1858, the Supreme Court of the United States invalidated two-thirds of his land grants on a technicality, and in 1865 his house was leveled by an arsonist.

Sixty-two years old, desperate for money, and convinced that the United States Government was responsible for his plight, Sutter moved to Washington, D.C., where he became a kind of squatter himself. For over fourteen years he appealed to Congress for reimbursement. For over fourteen years bills were introduced on his behalf in session after session, but always Congress procrastinated. After the first five years of lobbying, sick of hotel and boardinghouse life, he and his wife built a house at Lititz, Pennsylvania, in the heart of the German settlements, where they lived for the rest of their lives. They kept to themselves, too proud to endure the curiosity of their neighbors.

In June 1880, crippled by rheumatism, Sutter trudged to Washington for the last time, hopeful to the end for relief; but Congress adjourned, the latest "Bill for the Relief of John A. Sutter" still in the hopper. Broken-hearted, Sutter died two days later in his hotel room, an unfinished letter to his wife on the table. His death certificate lists the immediate cause, misspelled but grimly accurate, as "exaustion."

GENL. JOHN A. SUTTER.
BORN FEB. 28TH 1803.
AT KANDERN. BADEN.
DIED JUNE 18TH 1880.
AT WASHINGTON. D.C.
REQUIESCAT IN PACEM.

Calvin Nathaniel Payne
(1844–1926)
OIL EXPERT

Woodlawn Cemetery
Titusville, Pennsylvania

In 1859 the first American oil well was brought in at Titusville, Pennsylvania; the following year John D. Rockefeller began buying up properties in the area; and by the mid-eighties his Standard Oil Trust controlled over 80 percent of the nation's production.

"Buy brains," Rockefeller urged, and in 1885 Standard Oil hired Calvin N. Payne, who was born near Titusville and had been operating in the oil industry since the age of fifteen. Payne became Standard's production expert, visited all the oil fields in the United States as well as in Russia, Rumania, Borneo, and Sumatra, and prospered. He retired in 1911, died of old age in his eighty-third year, and was buried in Titusville in the very ground that brought forth the nation's first petroleum.

We feel a special affection for Calvin Payne, not for his successes, which were considerable, but for the notion that, if you're going to make a mistake, make it a big one. Just after the turn of the century, when he was at the height of his career, Standard Oil sent him to investigate a suspicious mound called Spindletop, near Beaumont, Texas. He sniffed around the mound, saw nothing that he had ever seen before, yawned, and reported back to the company that he found "no indication whatever to warrant the expectation of an oil field on the prairies of southeastern Texas."

CALVIN NATHANIEL PAYNE
BORN MAY 25, 1844 — DIED SEPT. 13, 1926
MARTHA DEMPSEY
WIFE OF CALVIN N. PAYNE

Agitators and Reformers

Whether winning or losing, the American mind is not a complacent mind. To believe in something, to hold to that belief, is an American characteristic that continues to produce extremes. These people were bent on agitation or reform. They represent the variety of American enthusiasms.

Henry David Thoreau

(1817–1862)
ECCENTRIC

*Sleepy Hollow Cemetery
Concord, Massachusetts*

Henry Thoreau promulgated the art of copping out long before "flower children" carried daisies in protest and fled the cities for the simple life. The standard references describe him variously as a writer, author, essayist, poet, naturalist, transcendentalist, and philosopher, but we prefer to remember this jack-of-all-trades as a gentle eccentric, a kook.

He was christened David Henry but reversed the names because he thought they sounded better. At Harvard he wore a green coat when the regulations required black. His career as a public school teacher ended abruptly when, stung by criticism that he was sparing the rod and spoiling the children, he arbitrarily flogged a handful within an inch of their lives and then resigned. As a protest against slavery he refused to pay his poll tax and was put in jail, where his friend Ralph Waldo Emerson visited him and asked, "Why are you in there, Henry?" "Why are you out there?" Thoreau replied.

His attacks on slavery, his celebrated essay "Civil Disobedience," and his spirited defense of John Brown, earned him the reputation of a civil libertarian and reformer, but we think his significant contribution was his insistence on simplicity as an alternative to the urban complexities of what he called our "lives of quiet desperation." "Simplify, simplify," he cried out in *Walden*, his masterpiece. Examine nature with the naked eye, not through a telescope or microscope. Do without the outward manifestations of wealth and your inner self will be enriched by it.

His attempts to earn money were aimless because he coveted no more than bare subsistence. When hard up, he dabbled as a surveyor or a handyman or in the family business of pencil-making. It was all very well for him to preach the joys of poverty, but even during his celebrated two years, two months, and two days in solitude at Walden Pond, "I may as well state that . . . I dined out occasionally," mostly at the Emersons' where he lived off and on for a number of years. He published only two books during his lifetime: *A Week on the Concord and Merrimack Rivers* sold less than two-hundred-and-fifty copies, and even *Walden* did not achieve full recognition until after his death.

Ravaged by tuberculosis, Thoreau died at the age of only forty-four. Near the end, a friend said, "You seem so near the brink of the dark river, that I almost wonder how the opposite shore may appear to you." Thoreau's whispered reply was, "One world at a time."

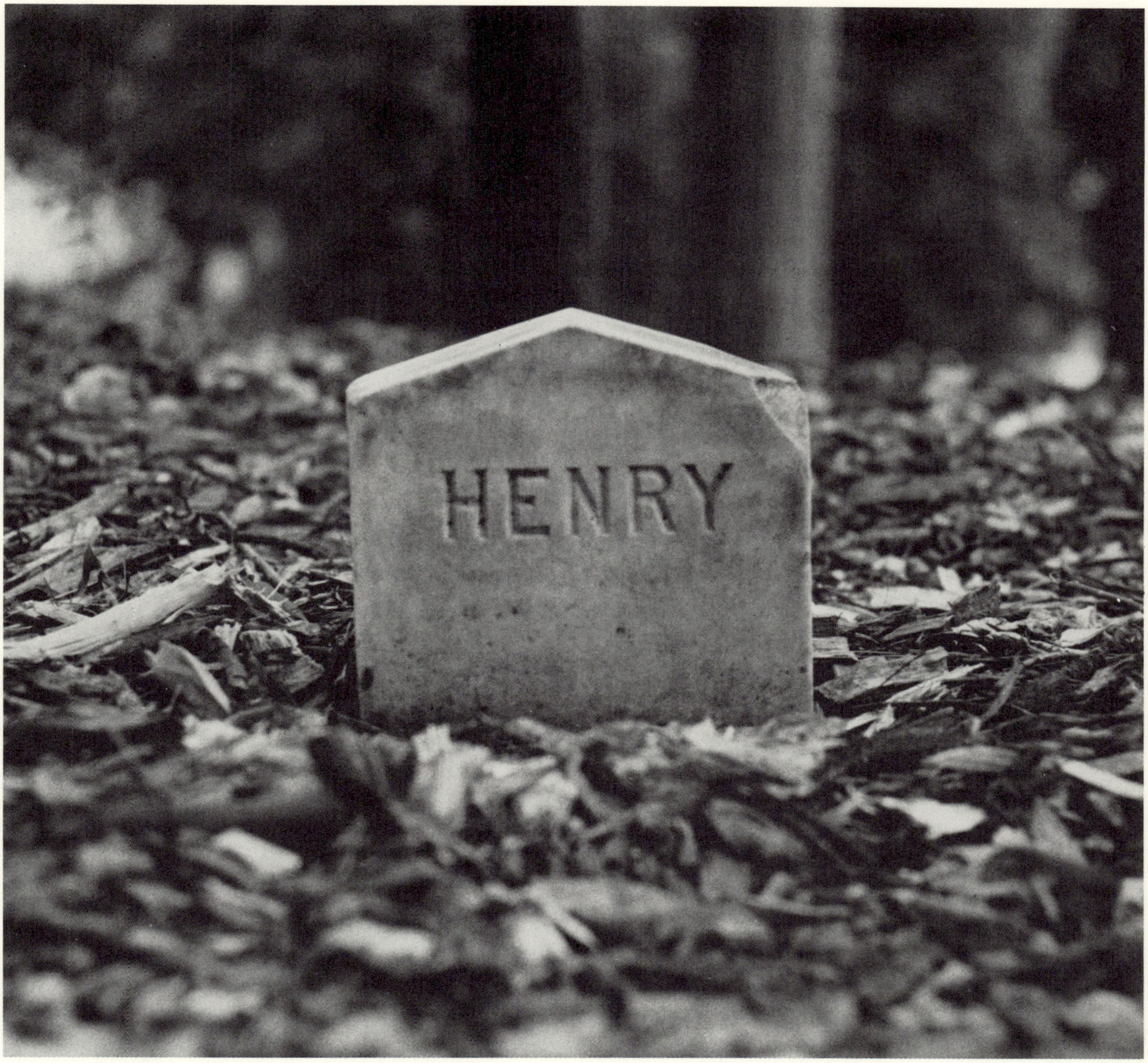
HENRY

CARRY A NATION
1846 – 1911

FAITHFUL TO THE CAUSE OF PROHIBITION
"SHE HATH DONE WHAT SHE COULD"

Carry Amelia Moore Nation
(1846–1911)
SALOON SMASHER

Belton Cemetery
Belton, Missouri

Carry Nation drew her first bead on John Barleycorn around the turn of the century when she took aim at Kansas drugstores, which could legally peddle alcohol for "medical, scientific and mechanical" needs. Enterprising druggists set up tables and kept ready-made prescriptions handy for those too sick to find the doctor. Soon the saloon smasher's battle cry of "Smash, women! Smash!" resounded farther afield. Although she did not live to see Prohibition, Carry's "hatchetations" whipped the temperance movement into a national ruckus.

Saloonkeepers quaked when this six-footer, a poke bonnet tied under her motherly chin, sailed into view to do "God's work." "Peace on earth, good will to men!" she roared, smashing bottles, shattering windows, and wrenching refrigerator doors from their hinges, as beer gushed from the hatchetated vats. "Who hath sorrow? Who hath woe?" she chanted, as cherry-wood bars succumbed to the rhythmic whacks of her axe. She usually vanquished the opposition, although one spirited group of bartenders organized a "seltzer brigade" and lined up to hose her back with fizz shot from bottles.

Mother Nation's smashing inevitably landed her in jail now and then. She paid fines (as she supported herself) by selling miniature hatchets as souvenirs, but not before haranguing fellow inmates to swear off booze. Many responded to her clarion call just to get her off their backs. In court, she produced her Bible to offer "Supreme Court citations," and once, when the prosecutor questioned her legal maneuvers, she snapped, "Shut your mouth, you perjurer. We're trying this case by divine law, not by Kansas law."

The word spread to New York City, where bars sported signs that said "Welcome all Nations but Carey [sic]." Finally the reformer bought a little house in Arkansas, whence she ventured in her last years for occasional smashings and lecture tours, during which she branched out from her favorite topic to include such other evils as prostitution and masturbation. Gradually she began to have trouble putting sentences together. One January she started a speech in Eureka Springs, Missouri, suddenly looked bewildered, put her hand to her cheek, whispered "I . . . have . . . done . . . what . . . I . . . could," and collapsed. Taken to a hospital in Leavenworth, Kansas, she lingered, and died several months later.

Carry's grave was only a weedy mound until 1923, when friends put up this granite marker. The Eighteenth Amendment had been in effect for three years, and speakeasies were doing a rip-roaring trade in the "Devil's Brew."

Henry Louis Mencken
(1880–1956)
JOURNALIST

Loudon Park Cemetery
Baltimore, Maryland

The boobus Americanus is a bird that knows no closed season," declared H. L. Mencken. Most of his working life was spent going after that bird and our native sacred cows with his own brand of gunshot: words. He left his prey zapped.

As newspaperman, critic, and essayist, Mencken leveled his sights on the "Yahoos of the Bible Belt," presidents, Prohibition, the Ku Klux Klan, "chautauqua orators," an occasional professor ("which is to say, a man devoted to diluting and retailing the ideas of his superiors"), and the "simian gabble of the crossroads." To return the fire was to throw canned peas at a giant.

Mencken's zest for words is obvious in his comic, pugilistic writings. But nowhere is it more evident than in the work he began before the First World War and completed after the second: *The American Language*, a scholarly (but not "professorial") history and exploration of the way we talk.

In 1948, Mencken reported his last national political convention. Not long after that, a stroke left him unable to read or write, and for eight years he lived as a semi-invalid in his row house on Hollins Street in Baltimore. Readers came in to keep him abreast of the American scene, and he was able to give instructions for the completion of his last book from notes made before his illness. Several days before his death, with publication of *Minority Report* pending, he said, "It will be nice to be denounced again."

One winter evening, after a quiet dinner with his brother and a friend, he went up to his room and listened to a symphony on the radio. During the night's quietest hours he died in his sleep of a coronary occlusion.

Mencken had once complained about the lack of a "suitable burial service for the admittedly damned," a class in which he included himself. The problem of an appropriate ritual for him was easily solved: There was none. A few friends gathered briefly at his house to see Mencken "off on his last journey." Later his ashes were buried next to those of his wife, who had died twenty years before.

The animal tracks over his grave would not bother Mencken in the least, unless, perhaps, they were dog tracks, for he gave dogs the same leveling treatment as he did any other American nuisance. His stone carries no epitaph, but he had composed one: "If after I depart this vale, you ever remember me and have thought to please my ghost, forgive some sinner and wink your eye at some homely girl."

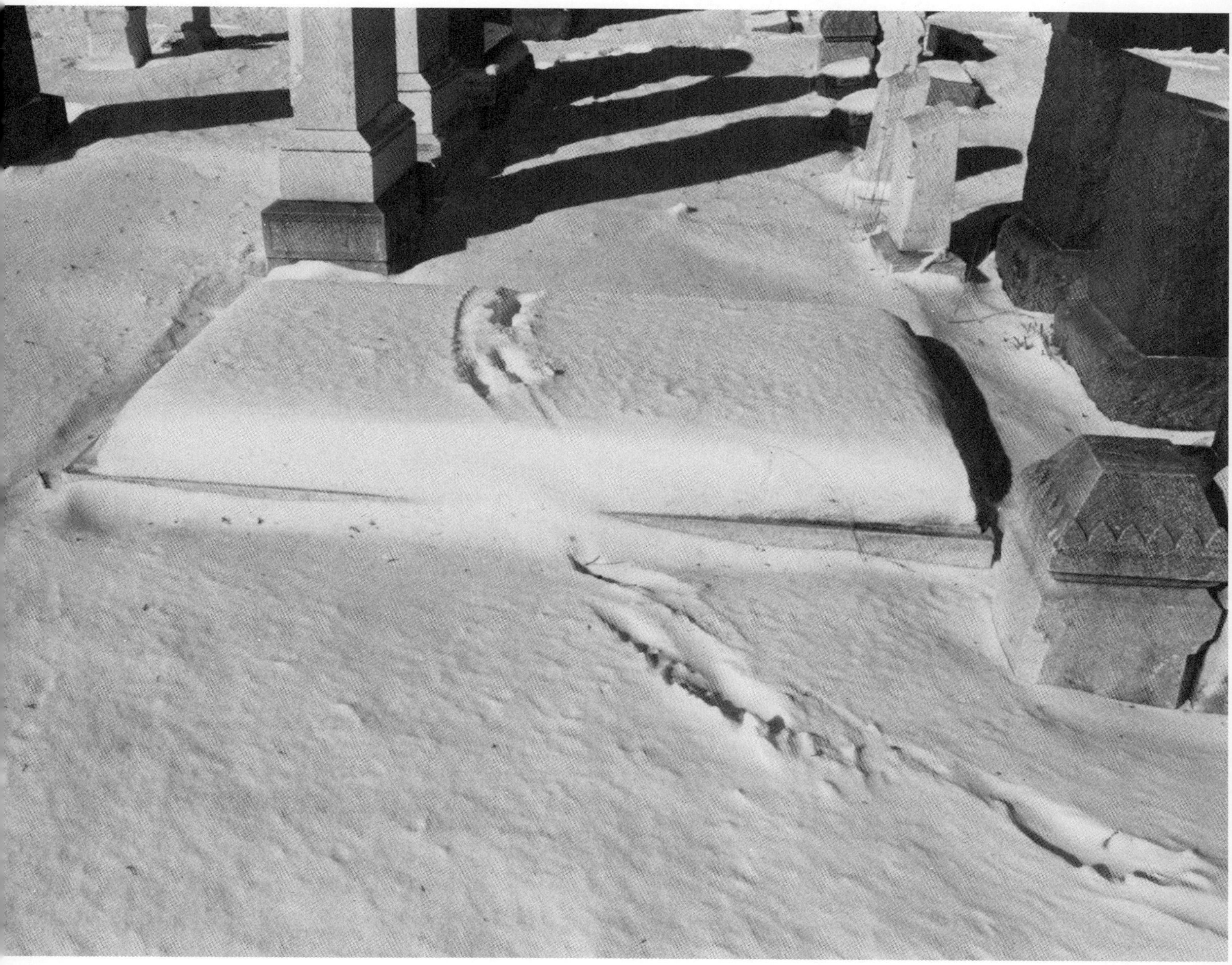

Martin Luther King, Jr.

(1929–1968)

CIVIL RIGHTS LEADER

Ebenezer Baptist Church
Atlanta, Georgia

Hundreds of thousands of people surrounded the Lincoln Memorial that bright August day when Martin Luther King, Jr., standing on the steps, abandoned his written text for the inspired words, "I had a dream . . ." Everyone was silent when he ended his speech with a line from a Negro spiritual: "Free at last! Free at last! Great God A'mighty, we are free at last!" No one foresaw, on that triumphant day, that the "moral leader of the nation" had spoken his own epitaph.

Five years later, after the funeral service at the Ebenezer Baptist Church, during which the meek and the powerful stood crushed together in the aisles, King's African-mahogany coffin was placed on the rough-hewn planks of a sharecropper's cart. Thousands followed as two mules pulled it several miles through the hot Atlanta streets to Morehouse College for a second ceremony.

King was buried temporarily beside his grandparents in South View Cemetery, founded after the Civil War by six Negroes so that the black community would no longer have to take its dead to the back gates of white cemeteries. Later he was moved and placed in this permanent tomb of white Georgia marble next to the Ebenezer Baptist Church, where King was co-minister with his father and where he had preached many times. In an elevated park surrounded by a reflecting pool, the tomb is part of the proposed site for the Martin Luther King, Jr., Center for Social Change.

REV. MARTIN LUTHER KING, JR.
1929 — 1968
"Free at last. Free at last.
Thank God Almighty
I'm Free at last."

Naturalists

The American vision has always included the bountiful land. These naturalists helped to give us a sense of its richness and how to use it.

John Chapman (Johnny Appleseed)

(1774–1845)
PIONEER

City Utilities Park
Fort Wayne, Indiana

The Swiss Lake Dwellers cultivated a small crab apple in the Bronze Age. The Greeks told a legend about the Apple of Discord, which led to the Trojan War. Traditionally, "an apple a day keeps the doctor away," and most of the apple trees in the Midwest flourish today because of John Chapman, the "Johnny Appleseed" of American folklore.

John Chapman was the prototype of the beatific hippie. As a youngster in Massachusetts, he was, according to legend, a child of nature, exploring and observing in the woods. When he left home, he traveled first to Pennsylvania and by the age of twenty-five was in north-central Ohio with a load of rotting apples—and their seeds—from Pennsylvania cider presses. There he began a primitive recycling job by planting orchards in small clearings in the wilderness and traveling barefoot to isolated cabins, giving apple seeds to settlers in exchange for food, old clothes, or IOUs, which he never claimed.

A wiry, exotic, ragtag apparition, Chapman was nonetheless welcomed by the struggling frontier families. He carried a bedroll and Bible with him and declaimed Swedenborgian revelations from a lotus position upon the floor. He sometimes wore a cooking pot as a hat. This visionary, charged with a sense of mission, was a kindly soul, compassionate toward Indians, settlers, and the small beasts of the wild country then being tamed. He could not kill a living creature for food, or harm an insect, or cut a tree.

His restless calling eventually took Chapman into Indiana; and there, after forty-six years of roaming, he caught pneumonia and died in a settler's simple frontier cabin north of Fort Wayne.

The crude stone marking his grave lies behind a rusty iron fence, atop a little knoll in a city park on the outskirts of Fort Wayne. It overlooks the Allen County War Memorial Coliseum, a modern concrete edifice not devoted to the pursuit of arboriculture. The St. Joseph River meanders nearby, floating an occasional apple blossom downstream to the Ohio.

"JOHNNY
APPLESEED"
JOHN CHAPMAN
HE LIVED FOR OTHERS
HOLY BIBLE
1774 – 1845

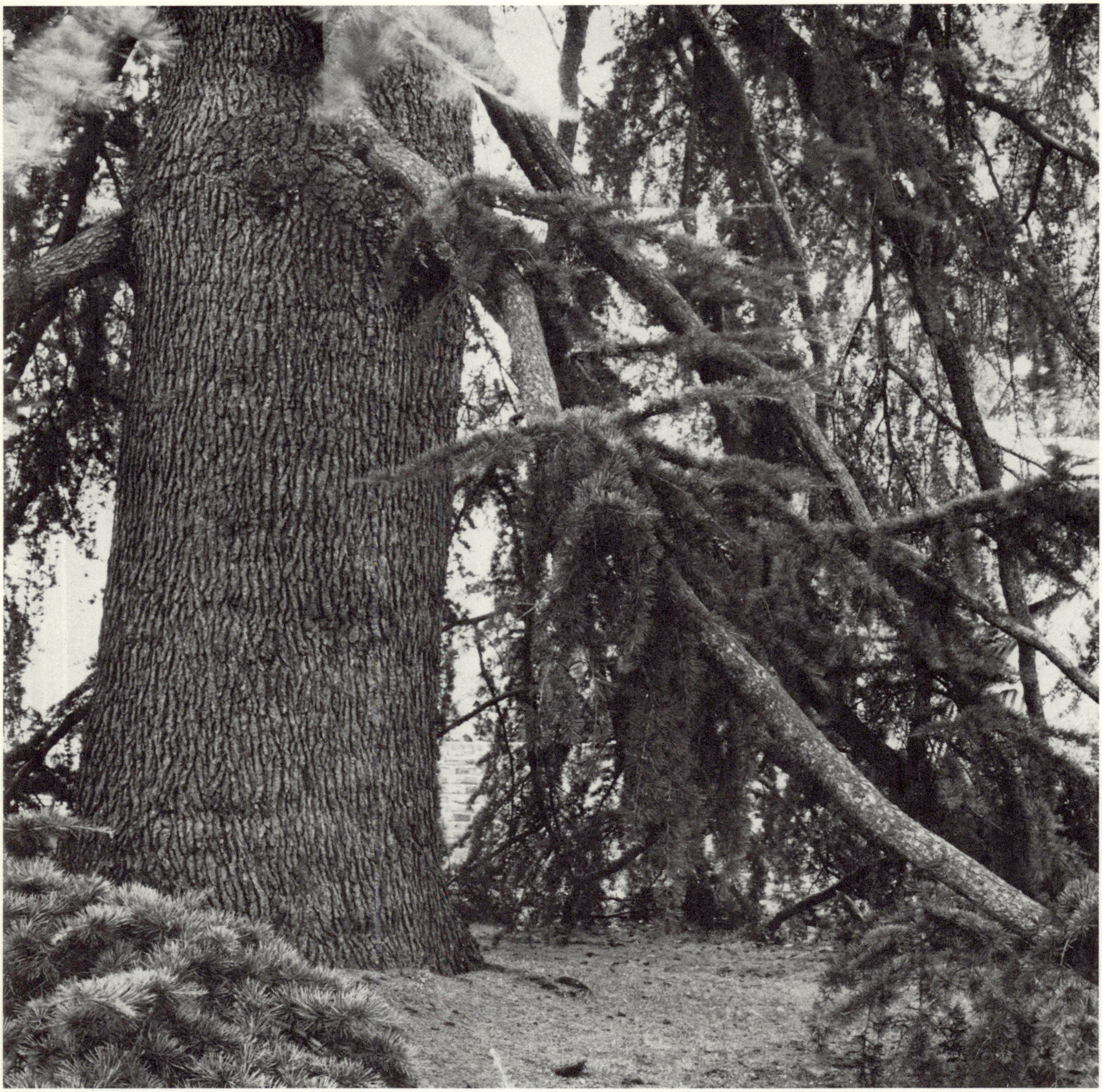

Luther Burbank

(1849–1926)

HORTICULTURIST

Luther Burbank Memorial Gardens
Santa Rosa, California

Luther Burbank was a harmless crank to some, and to others the greatest breeder of plant life the world has ever known. He had no formal scientific training in the modern sense and, unlike John Chapman, he was behind his times, albeit through no fault of his own. It has been said that, if he had lived fifty years earlier, Burbank might have been regarded as the father of American horticulture. As it was, his amateur experiments were overtaken by the rising tide of the science of genetics, but he still remains the pragmatic architect of many of our modern techniques of cultivation of the soil.

As a young man on a farm in Massachusetts, Burbank gained firsthand knowledge of the mysteries of plant life and developed his first innovation and one of his most important, the Burbank potato. At the age of twenty-six, he sold all his rights to the potato for one-hundred-and-fifty dollars to raise fare to California, which he regarded as "the chosen spot of all this earth as far as Nature is concerned." He purchased a tract of land in the Sonoma Valley, north of San Francisco, where he spent the rest of his life pursuing the gentle creative work that earned him the reputation as "the Edison and Ford of horticulture." His particular genius was in creating, recognizing, and selecting desirable plant variations and in reducing the length of time needed to develop the new seedlings by grafting them onto mature stock.

Near the end of his life, Burbank referred to himself as an "infidel," which got him into a peck of trouble with the fundamentalists of the day. "One Bryan," one of them thundered, "is worth a million Burbanks to any world, and the Bible will be doing business when you and your flowers are blowing down the years." But Burbank bore their abuse with serenity, puttering in his garden perfecting a new strain of his famed Shasta daisy. One spring evening he suffered a heart attack and became so afflicted with hiccups that he was unable to eat and wasted away in less than three weeks.

At his express request, his remains were interred under the enveloping limbs of this cedar of Lebanon near his greenhouse, a fitting monument to the man who made living things grow tall. His gardens, open to the public, have been so crudely vandalized that his horizontal bronze marker has been deliberately covered with turf.

George Washington Carver
(1864?–1943)
AGRONOMIST

Tuskegee Institute
Tuskegee, Alabama

George Washington Carver, whose parents were slaves and who was himself once exchanged for a three-hundred-dollar racehorse, never knew exactly how old he was. His propensity for investigating how things grow began when, as a frail child, he began observing and drawing plants and insects, ultimately to become his life's work. Thanks to him, the peanut, the sweet potato, and the soybean freed the South from its one-staple cotton economy and renewed its soil. Carver developed several hundred peanut by-products, including synthetic rubber, dyes, and a coffee substitute used by GIs in World War II.

He worked in his laboratory at Tuskegee Institute for over forty-six years. Even after hospitalization in 1937 for pernicious anemia, and later with a weakened heart and breathing trouble, he continued in his bailiwick, surrounded by bundles of letters, which arrived in such numbers that he couldn't keep up with them. Sometimes he would open a couple when he needed a little money, knowing his well-wishers often sent him a few dollars when they could.

His students worried about him, and Carver protested when they took to peeking into his lab to make sure he was all right. If he had wanted someone interrupting him all day, he joked, he would have married.

One evening Carver settled back on his bed pillows in his quarters on the college campus and said, "I think I'll sleep now." He died in his sleep a short time later. After a funeral service in the Institute chapel, he was buried near Booker T. Washington, the founder of Tuskegee, who had originally invited him there many years before. Today, around this corner, there still bustles the life of the college Carver helped make famous. His flat stone is almost part of the soil. And his epitaph, unlike so many, tells the "bare truth," which Lowell said would make an honest man "easier in his grave."

GEORGE WASHINGTON CARVER
DIED IN TUSKEGEE ALABAMA
JANUARY 5, 1943
A LIFE THAT STOOD OUT AS A GOSPEL OF
SELF-FORGETTING SERVICE.
HE COULD HAVE ADDED FORTUNE TO FAME
BUT CARING FOR NEITHER HE FOUND HAPPI-
NESS AND HONOR IN BEING HELPFUL TO
THE WORLD.
THE CENTRE OF HIS WORLD WAS THE SOUTH
WHERE HE WAS BORN IN SLAVERY SOME
79 YEARS AGO AND WHERE HE DID HIS
WORK AS A CREATIVE SCIENTIST.

Molders of the Land

Man's impact on the American landscape, "from sea to shining sea," has often been more destructive than ennobling. These men had different aspirations.

Pierre Charles L'Enfant
(1754–1825)
ARCHITECT, ENGINEER

Arlington National Cemetery
Arlington, Virginia

Standing before Pierre L'Enfant's grave, looking out over the city of Washington, D.C., we are reminded of the epitaph on the wall above Sir Christopher Wren's tomb in the crypt of St. Paul's Cathedral: *Si monumentum requiris circumspice*—"If you would see his monument look around you." As Wren's magnificent cathedral is his own monument, L'Enfant's is the graceful minuet of avenues, parks, circles, and squares he designed for our nation's "permanent seat on the bank of the Potowmac."

L'Enfant came to America at the age of twenty-three to fight in the Revolution, achieving the rank of major. Just when and how he received his training in architecture and engineering is not clear, but in 1791 he was commissioned to survey and lay out the site of the new "Federal City" on the Potomac, which he insisted should be "proportioned to the greatness which . . . the Capitale of a powerful Empire ought to manifest. . . . Having first determined some principal points to which I wished making the rest subordinate, I next made the distribution regular with streets at right angle, North-South and East-West, but afterwards I opened others on various directions, as avenues to and from every principal place." His innovative street plan confuses tourists to this day, but lends to the city an airy grandeur.

Once his plan was approved, L'Enfant set about executing it with a zeal so ferocious that he rubbed more and more people the wrong way until, finally, intolerably insubordinate and offensive even to George Washington himself, he was discharged. His claim for a fee of ninety-five thousand dollars was rejected, and his masterpiece earned him less than 10 percent of that sum. Later, approached to lay out what is now Paterson, New Jersey, L'Enfant conceived of "a plan . . . which far exceeds anything of the kind yet seen in this country," but his fee was again rejected as too high and the plan never came to fruition. Today, but for the sake of saving a few thousand dollars, Paterson might be comely instead of homely.

Bearing with equanimity the antagonisms that men ahead of their time often endure, L'Enfant died penniless at a friend's estate in Maryland and was buried there in an unmarked grave. In 1909, following a resurgence of interest in completing his plan after years of helter-skelter growth, Washington joined with the nation in honoring him. His remains were disinterred, laid in state in the Capitol, and then reinterred across the river, on a hillside overlooking his beautiful city, its design reproduced on his slab. Only one thing is wrong: L'Enfant could not foresee the patterns of modern traffic, and today the honking horns of rush hour sound an ironic knell to his memory.

PIERRE CHARLES L'ENFANT·
ENGINEER·ARTIST·SOLDIER·
VNDER THE DIRECTION OF
GEORGE WASHINGTON
ESIGNED THE PLAN FOR THE
FEDERAL CITY·

John Muir

(1838–1914)
ECOLOGIST

Muir Ranch
Martinez, California

A simple thistle decorates the grave of John Muir, but the trees, valleys, and cliffs of our national parks and forest reserves stand as a testimonial to his life's work. Geology, botany, and the pull of freedom from "the doleful chambers of civilization," impelled him to be a wanderer. He hiked in the Midwest and Canada, walked from Indianapolis to the Gulf of Mexico; and as he traveled he recorded his reflective observations of nature.

He drifted into California, where he was married in the ranch house near the graveyard where he is now buried. He worked at horticulture, but his greatest loves were places such as the wilds of Alaska, where he discovered a glacier, the unique Petrified Forest, and especially the Yosemite Valley. The mountains revitalized him, and when he found a railroad, sheep, or logging company staking out its "sore, sad center of destruction," he did not stand still. Through his journals, articles, and letters he aroused the public and influenced legislation to protect the wilderness for "the thousands needing rest—the weary in soul and limb, toilers in town and plain, dying for what these grand old woods can give."

Today, new houses spring up around the old ranchhouse, motorcyclists execute "wheelies" outside the fence, and rock music permeates the adjacent pear orchard. But Muir wanted to be buried next to his wife there by their home, for as the gentle man remarked in the Scottish brogue of his forebears, "Evenin' brings a' hame."

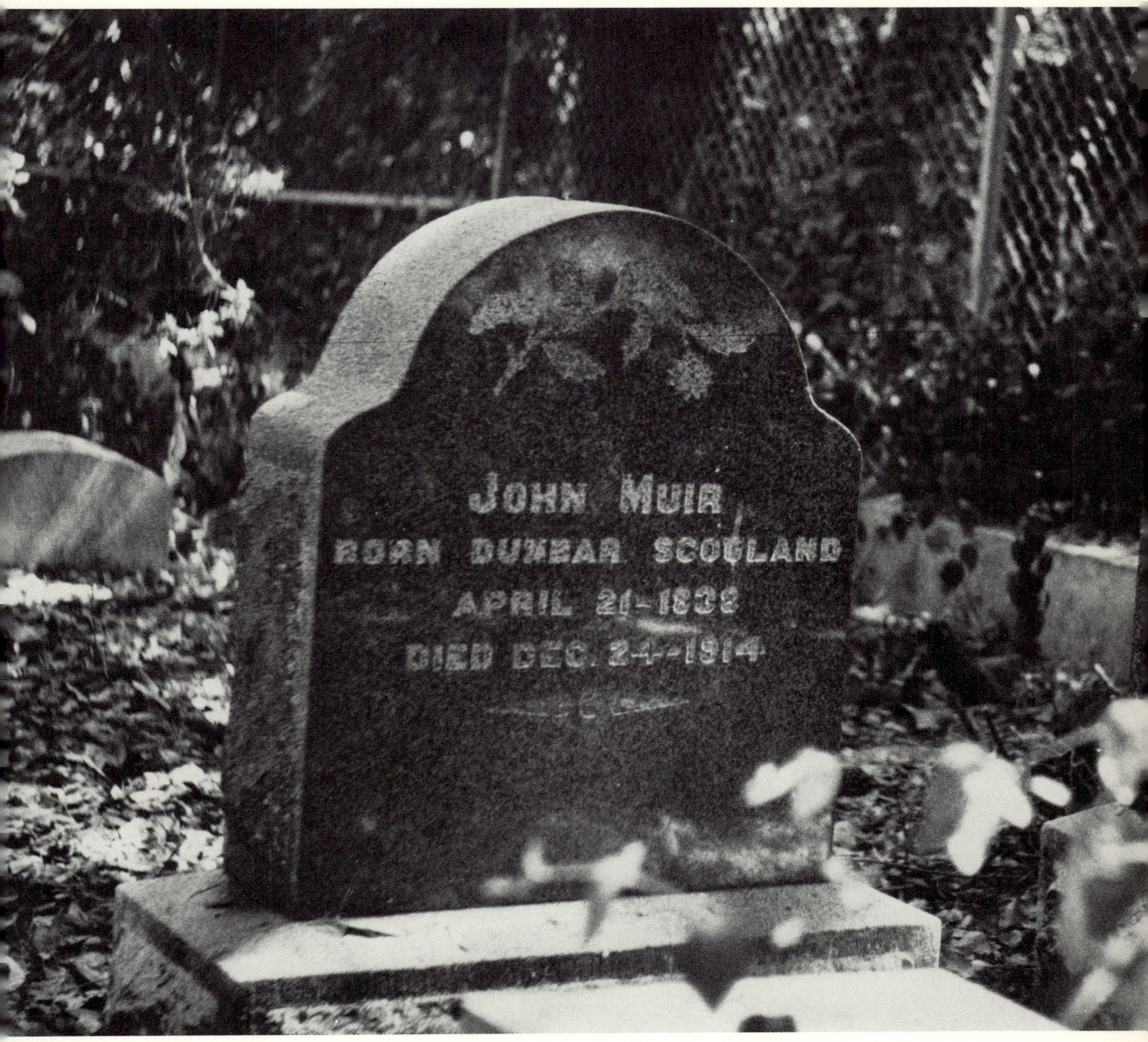
JOHN MUIR
DIED DEC. 24-1914

Performers

The mysteries of the inner and the outer man meet upon a stage. The result is that performers often become mythologized, off-stage objects of a cult or devotion. These people had that certain aura.

Edwin Thomas Booth

(1833–1893)
ACTOR

*Mount Auburn Cemetery
Cambridge, Massachusetts*

Like the Barrymores a generation later, Edwin Booth was born into an acting family. His father was one of the giants of the nineteenth-century Shakespearean stage: and his younger brother, John Wilkes Booth, was a promising actor—before achieving recognition in a different way at Ford's Theater in Washington.

Edwin Booth was the first and one of the greatest American tragedians. He also knew the baleful drama fate could inflict offstage: the death of his first wife less than three years after their marriage, leaving him with a two-year-old daughter; his brother's assassination of Lincoln, which forced him into a long retirement; the loss of his theatrical library and extensive collection of scenery, costumes, and portraits in a fire at the Winter Garden in New York; his second wife's insanity and death; the bankruptcy and closing of Booth's Theater, which he had built and animated; and the slow but inexorable deterioration of his body during the last twenty years of his life.

Enfeebled by a brain hemorrhage, Booth spent his last days on a diet of milk, the only nourishment he could hold down. He died during one of Manhattan's first power blackouts. At the same instant his casket was being carried out of the Little Church Around the Corner in New York, three floors collapsed in Ford's Theater, killing a score of persons.

The quotation on the reverse side of his monument (*see frontispiece*), attributed simply to "Shakespeare," has been subtly altered from the original (*Much Ado About Nothing*, IV: I: 226), converting it into a reflective message from the grave.

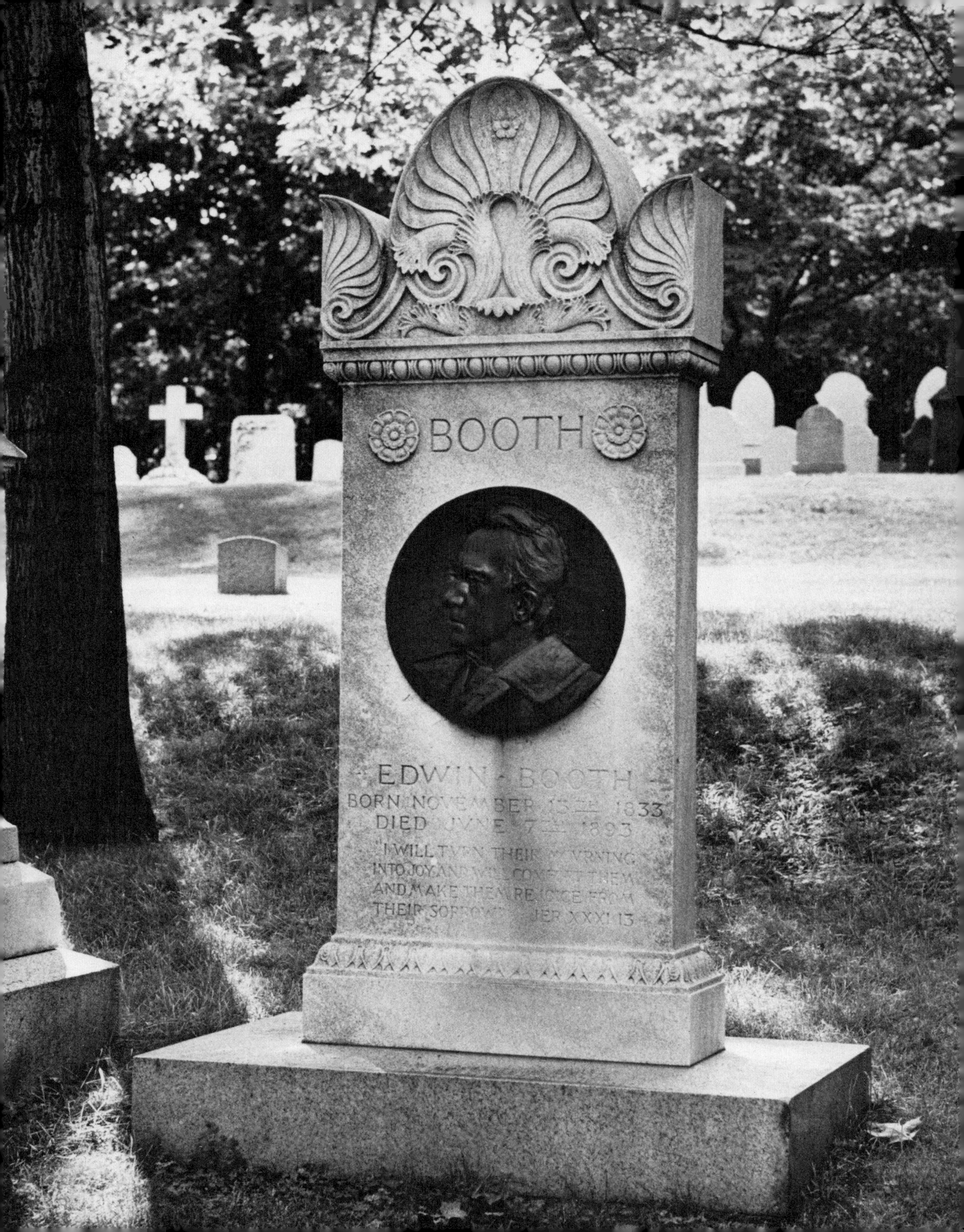
BOOTH
EDWIN BOOTH

Harry Houdini

(1874–1926)
MAGICIAN

*Machpelah Cemetery
Brooklyn, New York*

Ehrich Weiss was born in Hungary but grew up in, of all places, Appleton, Wisconsin. He changed his name to Harry Houdini; and it became synonymous with surprise, delight, and clean entertainment for millions of people.

Although generally acknowledged to be the greatest magician of all time, Houdini's main reputation was as an escape artist. No locks, no chains, no cells could hold him. He held a generation of Americans breathless, holding his own breath for seemingly impossible lengths while he extricated himself from all manner of buried or submerged containers, or wriggling out of straitjackets while suspended from cranes upside down over the heads of the gasping crowd.

On tour in Montreal in the fall of 1926, some McGill students engaged Houdini in a conversation about his ability to withstand hard blows without injury. One student, apparently taking him by surprise, punched him several times in the stomach. By the time the tour reached Detroit, Houdini was in agony. Hastily examined in his dressing room, he was found to have acute appendicitis, but Houdini, told that the theater was sold out, insisted on going on. His brave performance that evening, so paralyzed with pain that an assistant had to take over much of his act, was his last. After the curtain fell, he collapsed and was rushed to a hospital, where surgeons removed a ruptured and gangrenous appendix and found peritonitis badly advanced. But this man, who had so often defied death, hung on for a week. In the darkest and quietest hours of Halloween morning, he whispered to his brother, "I guess this thing's going to get me," and closed his eyes for the last time.

By grim coincidence, a great bronze coffin he had had specially built for one of his underwater escapes was accidentally left behind in Detroit when the troupe returned to New York after Houdini collapsed. He followed them in it. At the end of the funeral service at an Elks' clubhouse, a colleague broke a ceremonial wand, as Houdini had specified, over the coffin. This gesture later became the magicians' traditional good-bye. He was buried on a pillow of his mother's letters, beneath an elaborate monument he designed himself, surmounted by the granite bust, which can be seen in the picture, staring as if in disbelief at the locked gate of no escape. Fifty years after his death, there are still published reports that the inscriptions on the monument are an unsolved code to the location of a booby-trapped vault nearby, in which the master hid his secrets.

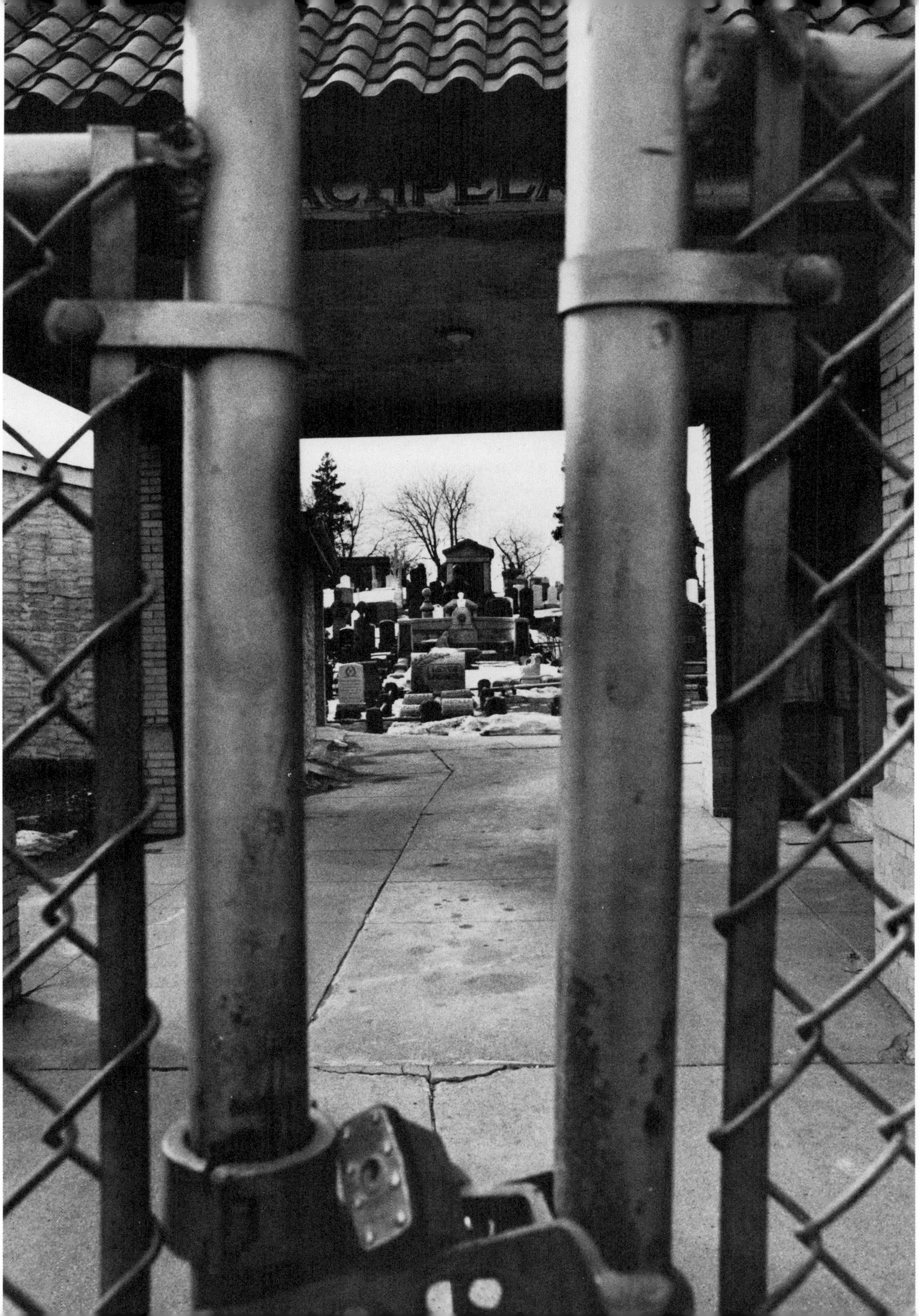

George Michael Cohan
(1878–1942)
SHOWMAN

*Woodlawn Cemetery
Bronx, New York*

What was so striking about George M. Cohan was his enormous versatility. Whether working as an actor, dancer, playwright, lyricist, composer, director, manager, or producer, his small, jaunty frame exuded boundless energy and exuberance. His self-deprecating "I'm just a song-and-dance man," and self-spoofing "I can write better plays than any living dancer and dance better than any living playwright," belied his vast talent.

Indisputably the most important theater figure of his time, his contributions to American entertainment included some fifty full-length plays, the most successful probably his dramatization of Earl Derr Biggers's mystery novel, *Seven Keys to Baldpate,* and more than five hundred songs, among them "Give My Regards to Broadway," "The Yankee Doodle Boy," and "It's a Grand Old Flag." His stirring World War I march, "Over There," became practically a national anthem and won him a congressional medal, presented at the White House by President Roosevelt, whom he impersonated in the Kaufman and Hart/Rodgers and Hart musical, *I'd Rather Be Right.* Best known as sovereign of the musical theater, Cohan demonstrated equal talent as a serious actor in another of the few plays he appeared in written by someone else, Eugene O'Neill's *Ah, Wilderness!*

Cohan appeared in his last play in 1940. In July 1941 his longtime partner, Sam H. Harris, died of intestinal cancer, and by cruel coincidence Cohan began to develop symptoms of the same disease. In October he had an operation, and another in January, which revealed that the cancer had spread beyond retrieve. "The man who owned Broadway" gave his last regards to it one supremely private summer evening in 1942, when he sat quietly in the back of a darkened movie theater and enjoyed a few minutes of *Yankee Doodle Dandy,* the newly released film of his life, starring James Cagney. On November 4, he slipped into a coma. Among his last words, to his crony Gene Buck, were "No complaints, kid" (he called everyone "kid"). He received the last rites of the Roman Catholic Church and died at dawn the next day, holding his daughter's hand. As the casket was carried out of St. Patrick's Cathedral, the organ played "Over There" as a dirge. His churchlike mausoleum, designed by Tiffany, also harbors his father, mother, and sister with whom he shared his early vaudeville days as "The Four Cohans," and is only a few paces away from Sam Harris's.

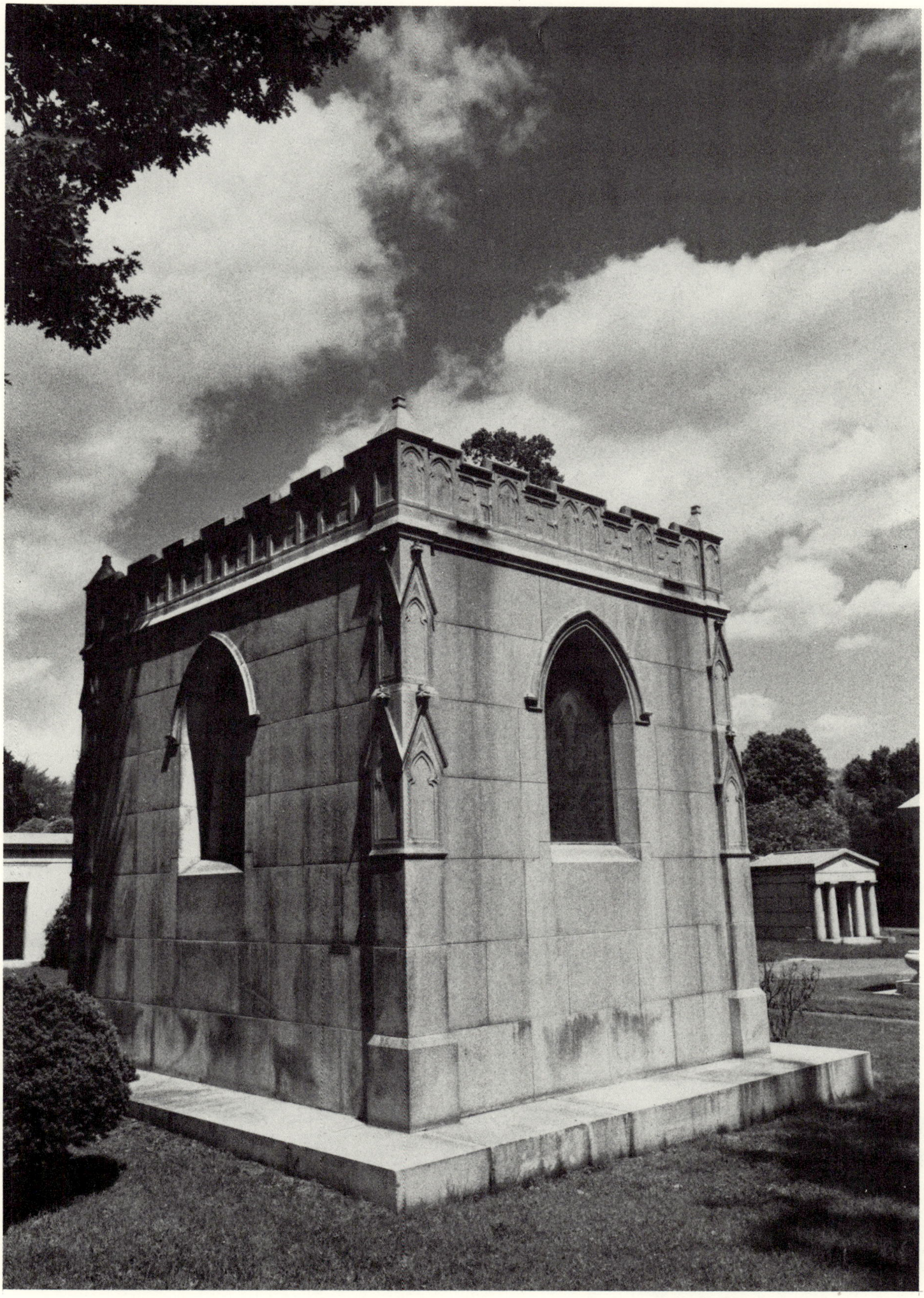

THE GREATEST BLUES SINGER
IN THE WORLD WILL NEVER
STOP SINGING
BESSIE SMITH
1895 —— 1937

Bessie Smith

(1895?–1937)
SINGER

Mount Lawn Cemetery
Sharon Hill, Pennsylvania

At the height of the blues craze in the 1920s, Bessie Smith had her own show and her own railroad car. By 1937, glad to be working at all, she was aiming for a comeback. Then, one night after a show, she set off by automobile for the town where she was to perform the next night. Her lover was at the wheel. Their car slammed into a truck, which was stopped on a dark and narrow road near Clarksdale, Mississippi. It was one-thirty in the morning.

Bessie lay moaning in the middle of the pavement as the taillights of the truck disappeared. It was never identified. A doctor arrived, by coincidence traveling the same stretch of road. Her right side was crushed, and she was in shock. By morning her right arm had to be amputated. According to the death certificate, she died at "Afro-American Hospital" in Clarksdale. Legend has it that she was taken to the white hospital, refused treatment because of her color, and bled to death as a result. Evidence to the contrary includes the black ambulance driver's statement (albeit twenty years later) that he had taken her to the black hospital. The two were less than half a mile apart.

The Queen of the Blues was laid out for viewing in the O. V. Calto Elks Lodge in Philadelphia, her adopted hometown. Ten thousand came to grieve as she lay in a lace dress in the shiny velvet-lined casket. At the funeral, a choir sang "Rest in Peace," professional pallbearers carried out the casket, and a thirty-nine-car cortege formed for the trip to Mount Lawn.

It was an expensive funeral, but no money was spent to mark her grave. Thirty-three years later, when some reissued recordings rekindled interest in her soul-striking talent, a young woman wrote a letter to the local press about the omission. Rock singer Janis Joplin paid half the cost of the five-hundred-dollar stone. The other half was paid by Juanita Green, Bessie's former household helper and friend. There is a certain poignancy about the stone today, standing large and apart, as if it were trying to bring back a little of the spell of the flaming days.

George Herman (Babe) Ruth
(1895–1948)
BASEBALL PLAYER

Gate of Heaven Cemetery
Hawthorne, New York

Babe Ruth, with his booming bat, made baseball into the collective American spectator sport. Six-feet-two-inches tall, barrel chested, spindly legged, he hit a record sixty home runs in 1927 and carried subsequent fame with aplomb, greeting swarms of admirers with a genial "Hello, kid" here, and a "How's it going, doc?" there. He was so idolized that during World War II propaganda exchanges, when the Americans taunted "To Hell with Hirohito!" the Japanese retorted "To hell with Babe Ruth!"

The Sultan of Swat was really a hulking kid with a cobweb-coated mind. The first time he stayed at a hotel, straight out of a school for wayward and orphaned boys, he rode the elevators up and down, up and down, delighting in the appurtenances of the outside world. He never lost a hedonistic sense of awe, and as this Great Blue Ox of baseball worked his way through the crowds, so he worked his way through bordellos, all-night victory celebrations, and so much food that he took bicarbonate of soda regularly before games. Fined five thousand dollars for "misconduct, drinking and staying out all night," he repented for a time, and then did it all over again. Twenty years later Hollywood immortalized the incident, but in the movie version he was late to a game because he had ministered to an injured dog.

Babe Ruth was already ill when the film was made; his last two years were spent in and out of a New York hospital. A severe facial pain proved to be caused by a malignancy that wrapped around his carotid artery. Surgery, radiation treatments, and drugs could not eradicate the disease. No one ever told him that he had throat cancer.

And so the all-American favorite, the southpaw who started off with a right-handed glove, ended up a frail invalid. The booming voice, which had hurled obscenities at hecklers, shrank to a raspy whisper. "Fine" and "Thanks very much" were about it from the player who still held fifty-four major-league records. Little boys, whose fathers had chased the balls he hit clear out of the stadium, tiptoed into the hospital lobby to ask how he was and to send up an occasional bouquet of flowers. When a hospital bulletin announced that he was "sinking rapidly," the photographers in the lobby started testing their equipment. The Babe always drew crowds, even in death.

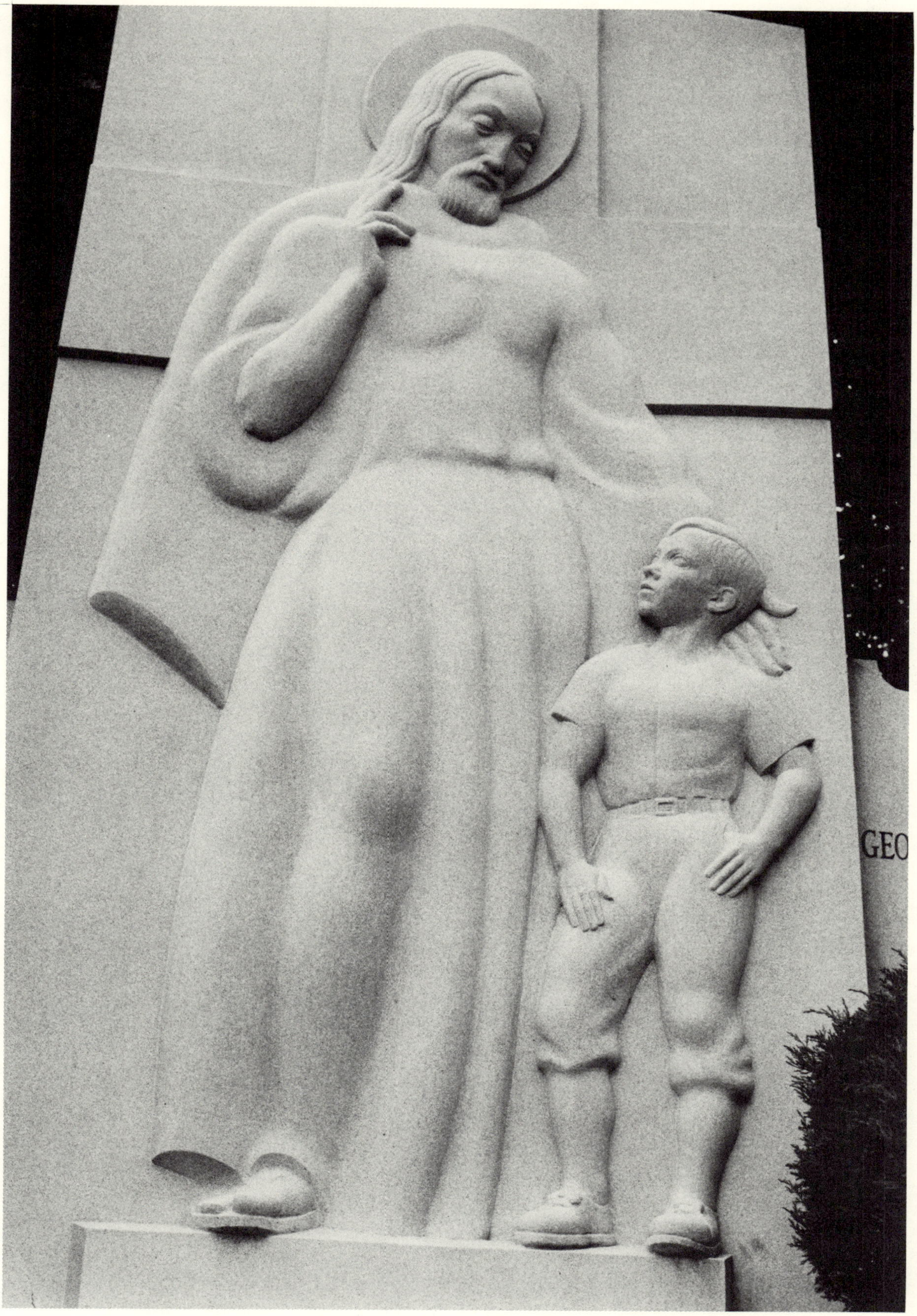
GEO

TALLULAH
BROCKMAN
BANKHEAD
JANUARY 31 1902
DECEMBER 12 1968

Tallulah Brockman Bankhead

(1902–1968)
ACTRESS

St. Paul's Episcopal Churchyard
Kent County, Maryland

Anyone of her era who had read *Gone With the Wind* but had not seen the movie would very likely have visualized Tallulah Bankhead as Scarlett O'Hara. So did Tallulah, and when producer David O. Selznick passed her over, Tallulah was, to put it mildly, teed off.

Sprung full blown from a distinguished Alabama political family (her grandfather and her uncle were United States Senators and her father was Speaker of the House of Representatives), she achieved Olympian heights in such plays as *The Skin of Our Teeth*, *The Little Foxes*, and *Private Lives*. But, ironically, she is remembered more for the role she played in her own private life: an insolent nose-thumber at the more traditional values of American life depicted elsewhere in these pages. Perhaps Billy Rose, whom she called a "loathsome little bully," best called her number when he retorted, "How can you bully Niagara Falls?"

What made this exquisite offspring of old Southern gentility tick? Rebellion? Frustration? Who knows. Her thirst for high living and high loving was legion, and she cheerfully admitted to being as "pure as the driven slush." Although she claimed she never missed a performance because of liquor, years of dissipation overtook her at the relatively young age of sixty-five, when she died of influenza, complicated by pneumonia. Her last words were "codeine . . . bourbon . . ."

She sleeps, almost profanely, in the churchyard of the oldest continuous Episcopal parish in Maryland, on the fashionable Eastern Shore near her sister's home, where she visited every summer. Her coffin is lined in her favorite baby blue, she is dressed in a cigarette-burned silk wrapper, and her father's good-luck rabbit foot is with her. If you listen carefully, you may hear in the honking of the Canada geese on the nearby lake her sleepless, honky "DAAHLING!"

Judy Garland
(1922–1969)
ACTRESS, SINGER

Ferncliff Cemetery
Hartsdale, New York

Judy Garland's fruitless search for happiness "over the rainbow" began as Frances Ethel Gumm in Grand Rapids, Minnesota, and ended forty-seven years later in a London bathroom. On the day she died a tornado swept over Kansas, and the tornado of her popularity sweeps on undiminished today.

What was remarkable about Judy was the dipole quality of her following. At one pole were the children of all ages who still delight in her peach-fuzz performance as Dorothy in *The Wizard of Oz*; ten-year-old Shirley Temple was MGM's first choice for the part, but they had to settle for sixteen-year-old Judy, heavily swaddled about the chest. "Over the Rainbow" was almost cut from the final print, but went on to win an Academy Award and become Judy's undisputed trademark.

At the opposite pole were the fanatics who idolized and adulated her as an adult, stomped and screamed at her stage appearances, and clung to her everywhere she went. Judy used to joke that when she died "the flags would fly at half-mast on Fire Island," but the suspicion that her own father had been a homosexual haunted her all her life.

Driven by a host of personal and physical problems, Judy drove herself to death in a whirlwind of five marriages, worldwide concert tours, sleeping pills, pep pills, diet medicines, and nerve tonics. To glimpse her picture toward the end of her life is a shattering experience: wrinkled and bloated, with bags under the heavily made-up eyes that still, somehow, never quite lost the coal-black luster of her youth. One June morning in London, her husband awoke to find that she was not in bed and the bathroom door was locked. Alarmed, he climbed out on the roof and broke through the window. Judy was slumped on the toilet, dead.

The verdict at the inquest was, with characteristic British reserve, "Accidental death by an incautious dose of barbiturates." Her body was brought back to New York, where an estimated twenty thousand people filed past the glass-enclosed coffin. Actor James Mason delivered the eulogy at the funeral chapel. "Judy's great gift," he said, "was that she could wring tears out of hearts of rock." Mourners sang "The Battle Hymn of the Republic" as the casket was borne out under a blanket of yellow roses and taken to Ferncliff, where it was placed in a crypt until a mausoleum could be built. Eight years later, when this picture was taken, it was still there, with a vase of fresh flowers and a card that said simply, "From the Judy Garland Fan Club."

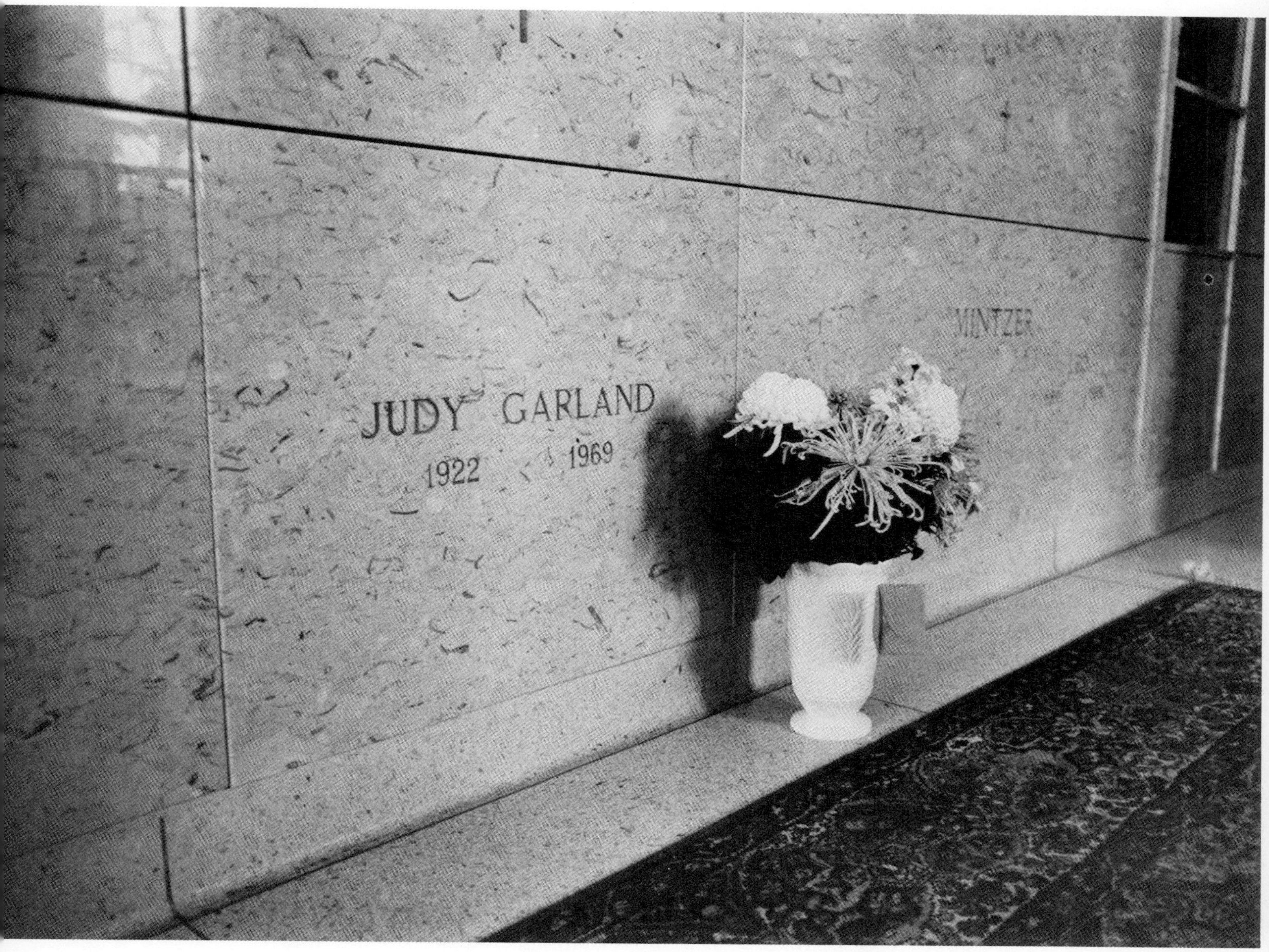
MINTZER
JUDY GARLAND
1922 1969

James Byron Dean
(1931–1955)
ACTOR

Park Cemetery
Fairmount, Indiana

James Dean is included in this collection because of the phenomenal hero worship that followed his death at the age of twenty-four. The young actor became a posthumous object of adoration.

He was a farm boy who liked motorcycles, and he became a Hollywood actor who liked fast sports cars. He bought a sixty-five-hundred-dollar Porsche Spyder and was checking it out, on his way to a race, when he collided with another car at a Y-shaped intersection near Paso Robles, California, and was killed instantly. The driver of the other car, traveling up the leg of the Y to make a left turn, was a college student on his way home for the weekend. He said at the hearing later that he had not seen Dean approaching from the right down a hill. Dean's speed was calculated by the police, who had given him a speeding ticket earlier the same afternoon, at eighty-six miles an hour.

Dean's body was flown back to his Indiana hometown. The undertaker in Fairmount ran a combination business—he kept caskets in the back of his furniture store. Dean was buried in one of these, and high school classmates served as pallbearers. Elizabeth Taylor, with whom he had just finished filming *Giant*, sent flowers.

The death of Jimmy Dean—who had played the rejected son, the outsider, the rebellious and misunderstood youth—was timely. People, mostly young people, identified with him. Teenagers dressed like him; some tried to drive like him. Mail-order merchants cashed in on the hero-worshipping craze; Dean's death inspired the sale of paraphernalia his followers could hold in their hands: wallet-sized photos, T-shirts, bits and pieces of silver paint and metal purportedly scraped from the wrecked Porsche. Movie magazines encouraged their readers with articles like "You Can Make Jimmy Dean Live Forever." Over six months after his death, a newspaper headlined a story, "Jimmy Dean Still Gets Mail." He did, even love letters. Some believers declared that he was going to rise again, while others pictured him as comfy where he was—as in the song, "Jimmy Dean's Christmas in Heaven."

The inanity reached even the burial ground. At his gravesite, admirers pecked away pieces of the stone for talismans. Although the intense fad was temporary, America's craving to hero worship is persistent.

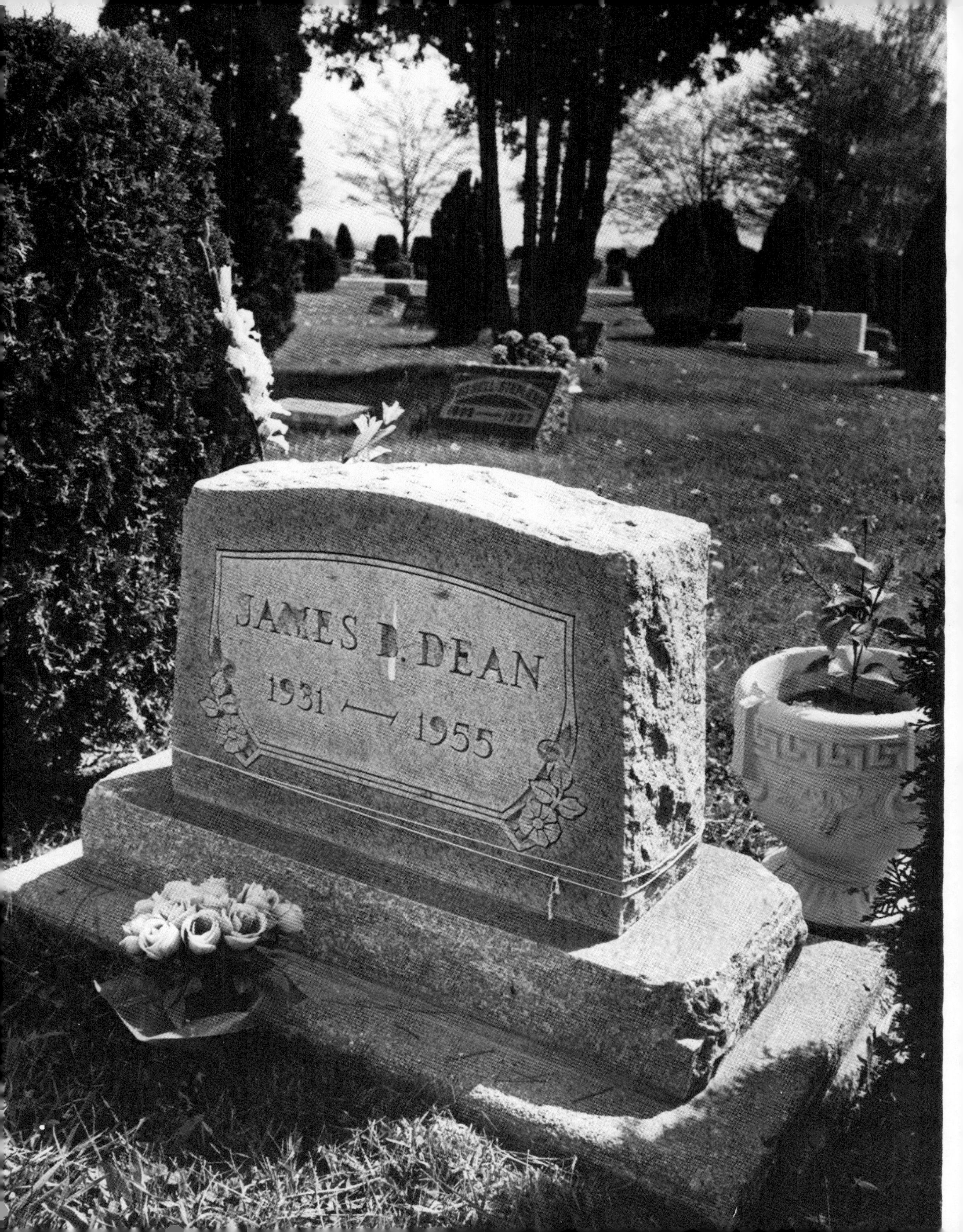
JAMES B. DEAN
1931 — 1955

Legends

There were real people who played tiny parts in larger scenes of historical moment. The kernels of their existence seeded ideas for legends, song, and verse, and their names are part of our folklore.

Barbara Hauer Fritchie
(1766–1862)
LEGENDARY PATRIOT

Mount Olivet Cemetery
Frederick, Maryland

> Up from the meadows rich with corn,
> Clear in the cool September morn,
> The clustered spires of Frederick stand
> Green-walled by the hills of Maryland . . .

The spires of Frederick really do cluster when viewed from the west, but John Greenleaf Whittier's famous poem made a heroine out of someone who really was not.

In the summer of 1863, one Emma Southworth, a Washington novelist, wrote to Whittier:

> When Lee's army occupied Frederick [September 6–10, 1862], the only Union flag displayed in the city was held from an attic window by Mrs. Barbara Frietchie, a widow lady, aged ninety-seven years.

Mrs. Southworth went on to describe how the Confederate troops, led by Stonewall Jackson, discharged a volley at the window, whereupon the old lady leaned out and cried, "Fire at this old head, then, boys; it is not more venerable than your flag!"

Whittier polished up the language with a little meter and rhyme:

> "Shoot, if you must, this old gray head,
> But spare your country's flag," she said.

He also thanked Mrs. Southworth for the idea. The poem appeared in the October 1863 issue of the *Atlantic Monthly,* and the rest is history.

History? True enough there was a real Barbara Fritchie, nee Barbara Hauer, who was born in Lancaster, Pennsylvania, on December 3, 1766, and died at Frederick on December 18, 1862, only three months after the Confederate occupation. At the age of forty she married John Caspar Fritchie, thus becoming, depending on which record you consult, Barbara Fritchie (the spelling that appears on the monument), Fritchee (the spelling in the cemetery deed), Frietchie (the form Whittier took from Mrs. Southworth's letter), Frietschie, Fritchy, Fritchey, Freitchie, or Fridshey.

An aged but enthusiastic patriot, Mrs. Fritchie probably waved the flag at the Union soldiers several days before when they marched through. The whole town did. But defy General Jackson his whole army? In fact, Jackson had been injured in a horseback accident on his way to Frederick and spent most of his time there recuperating in his tent. He was taken into town by ambulance once to attend church, where he fell asleep. On the morning the army moved out, he detoured through Frederick to leave a note at the home of a friend and then left by the shortest route to join his troops, passing near, but not directly by, Barbara Fritchie's house. It is unlikely that they ever even saw one another.

Ichabod B. Crane
(1787–1857)
MILITARY HERO

*Asbury Church of the Nazarene Cemetery
Staten Island, New York*

Washington Irving met Ichabod Crane when they were both stationed at Sackett's Harbor, New York, during the War of 1812. The name so tickled Irving's fancy that he helped himself to it several years later for the skittish schoolmaster in *The Legend of Sleepy Hollow*.

The real Ichabod Crane was no "affrighted pedagogue" with a frame "most loosely hung together," who gossiped his way into housewives' larders, sang through his nose, and whistled bravely to give himself courage when he heard tree branches creaking in the night. He was, in fact, the very opposite: a man of action, "tall and portly in appearance, dignified and agreeable in manner," and in his long military career he was noted for his integrity, honor, and heroism.

After Colonel Crane's death a marble shaft was placed over his grave, surmounted by the insignia—crossed cannons with the figure 1 above—of the First Regiment of Artillery, which he commanded. Meanwhile, in Sleepy Hollow, no one has ever been quite sure what happened to the trembling Ichabod after his encounter with the Headless Horseman, but legends have a way of living longer than military heroes.

SACRED
TO THE MEMORY OF
Col. ICHABOD B. CRANE
OF THE U.S. ARMY WHO WAS BORN
IN ELIZABETH TOWN, N.J.,
JULY 18th, 1787.
DIED ON STATEN ISLAND,
OCTOBER 5th, 1857.

HE SERVED HIS COUNTRY FAITHFULLY
48 YEARS AND WAS MUCH BELOVED
AND RESPECTED BY ALL WHO KNEW
HIM.

John Brown
(1800–1859)
ABOLITIONIST

John Brown Farm
North Elba, New York

The refrain that makes John Brown one of our national legends probably sprang up during the Civil War as a joke on quite another John Brown—a Yankee sergeant whose insubordinate regiment serenaded him to the tune of a well-known Sunday school hymn of the time. The tune achieved double-barreled immortality when Julia Ward Howe used it for "The Battle Hymn of the Republic," and when the Northern soldiers advanced to the contrasting irreverence of the refrain we know today:

> John Brown's body lies a-mouldering
>   in the grave,
> As we go marching on.

John Brown, the nonlegend, was a gaunt man with a flowing beard and penetrating blue-gray eyes, looking for all the world like a biblical patriarch. He came to upstate New York in 1849 to set up an agricultural community for freed blacks. His farm became a stop on the underground railroad and a home for his twenty children, but less frequently his own home, as the cause of abolition drove him to his destiny at Harper's Ferry.

Brown knew that in his death and martyrdom, his "truth" would go marching on. On the morning of his execution he handed his last message to a jailer: "I, John Brown, am now quite certain that the crimes of this guilty land: will never be purged away: but with blood. I had as I now think: vainly flattered myself that without verray much bloodshed; it might be done."

His wife was permitted to return his body to North Elba, after an appeal to the Virginia governor. "Put me in the shadow of the rock," Brown had requested—this huge boulder that darkens the weathered gravestone. The gravestone itself had been moved to the farm earlier, to use as a memorial for a son killed in 1856 during a Free-Soil skirmish. Before that, it had marked the Connecticut grave of Brown's grandfather, who fell early in the Revolution. Now, the country of his grandfather's time was older and about to be split by the agonies of civil war. Six days after Brown's execution, a fellow abolitionist remarked in eulogy at the graveside: "History will date Virginia Emancipation from Harper's Ferry." The bloodshed and the legend had begun.

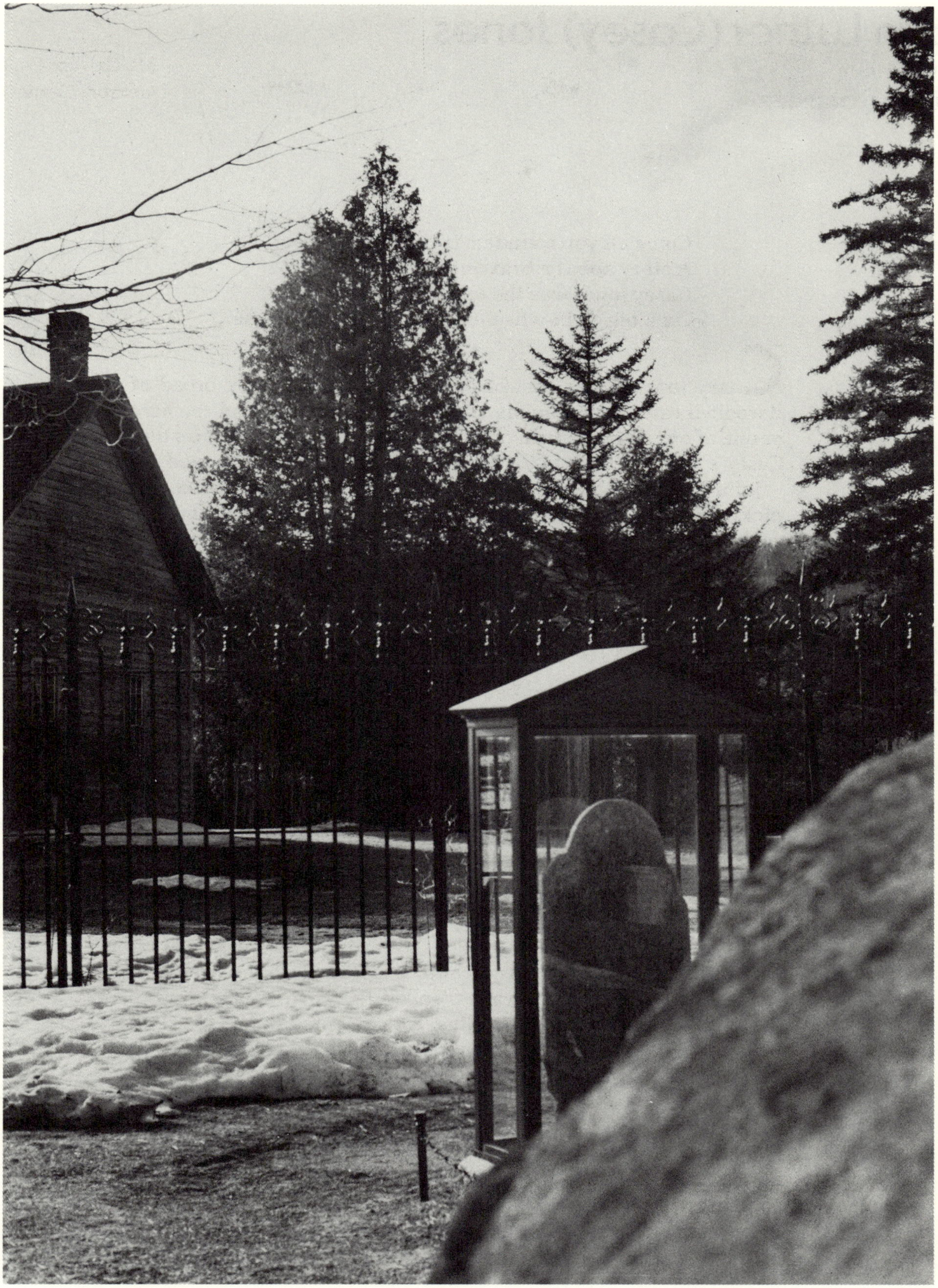

John Luther (Casey) Jones
(1864–1900)
RAILROAD ENGINEER

Mt. Calvary Cemetery
Jackson, Tennessee

> Come all you rounders if you want to hear
> A story about a brave engineer;
> Casey Jones was the rounder's name,
> On a big eight-wheeler, boys, he won his fame.

Casey Jones is our best-known symbol of the early breed of daredevil railroad engineers who laughed at death, and the hero of one of our most enduring ballads. But not everyone knows that Casey's "farewell trip to the Promised Land" really happened.

John Luther Jones hailed from Cayce, Kentucky, hence his nickname. He was a long, lean, lanky man, so tall that he couldn't stand up in the engine cab without sticking his head outside, reminding some of his friends of a young giraffe. Anyone could recognize Casey's six-tone calliope whistle, which he played like a musical instrument; it was said that he could make cold chills run up and down your spine with it.

> The switchman knew by the engine's moans
> That the man at the throttle was Casey Jones.

One night, in 1900, Casey was called to take the Illinois Central's Cannonball, running an hour and a half late, out of Memphis with orders to make up time. About one-hundred-and-seventy-five miles south, at Vaughan, Mississippi, two freight trains pulled into a siding to let Casey by, and discovered they were too long to clear the main line. Crewmen scrambled up the main line to put warning torpedoes on the track, but they barely managed to get out of the way when Casey shot around the curve at seventy miles an hour with his throttle wide open. When he heard the torpedoes he hit the brakes, yelled to his fireman to jump, and skidded into the protruding freight cars alone. He died instantly, with an unblemished record of never being involved in an accident that resulted in the death of a passenger or a fellow employee.

The clock stopped for Casey Jones at three fifty-two in the morning on April 30, 1900. That would have been the end of him, except that his engine wiper, Wallace Saunders, made up a chant about the accident, which was picked up and published by a professional songwriter under his own name. Wallace Saunders was quickly forgotten, but Casey Jones became immortal.

JOHN LUTHER
· JONES ·
1864 — 1900
TO THE MEMORY OF THE LOCOMOTIVE ENGINEER, WHOSE NAME AS 'CASEY JONES' BECAME A PART OF FOLKLORE AND THE AMERICAN LANGUAGE: 'for I'm going to run her till she leaves the rail– or make it on time with the southbound mail.'

THIS MEMORIAL ERECTED 1947 TO PERPETUATE THE LEGEND OF AMERICAN RAILROADING AND THE MAN WHOSE NAME BECAME ITS SYMBOL OF DARING AND ROMANCE — CASEY JONES

Stylemakers

When they are being objectionable, the English like to observe that Americans would relish a monarchy. Not true. What Americans do relish is someone to set a tone, to give substance to their dreams. These stylemakers tickled our appetite.

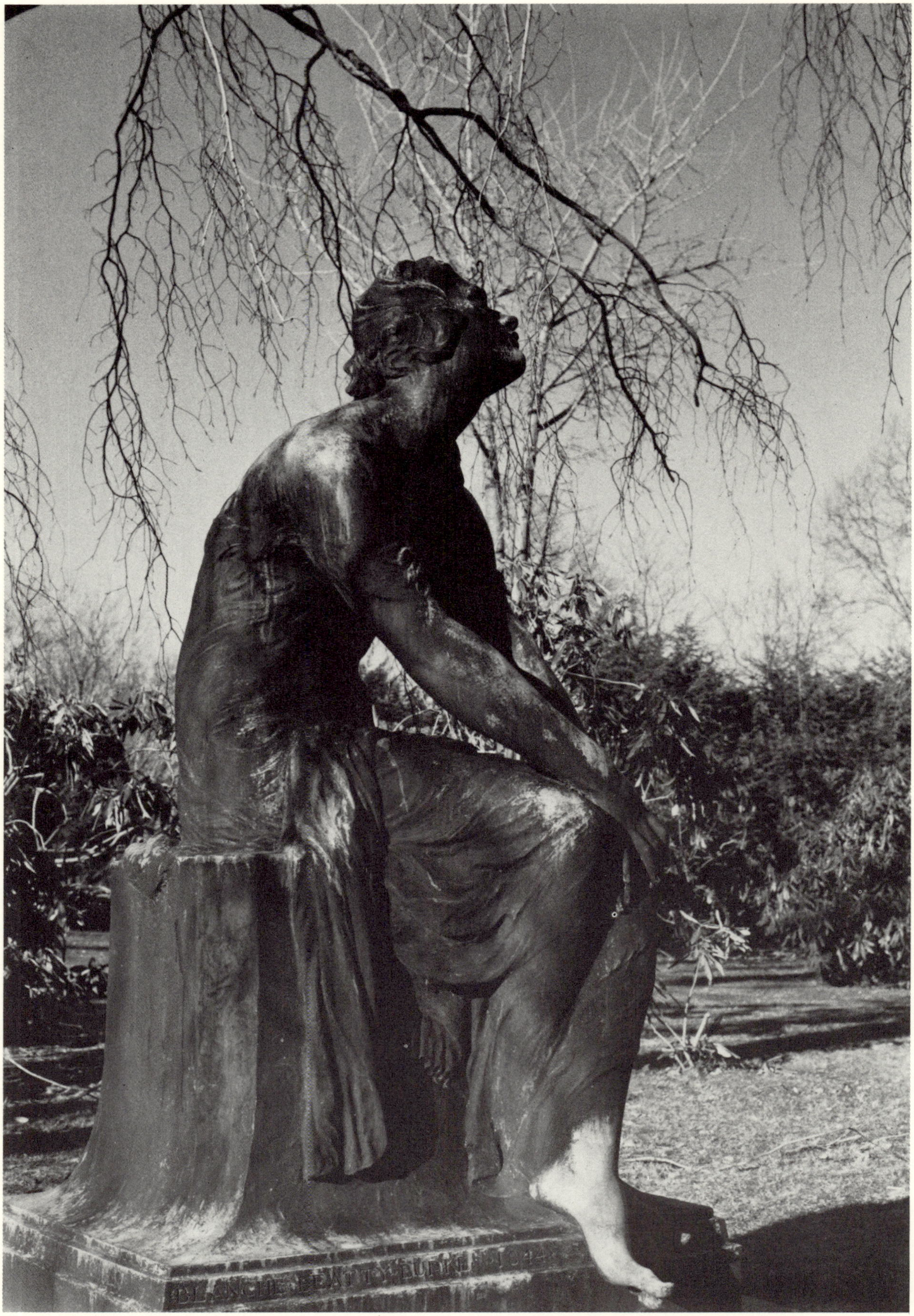

Florenz Ziegfeld, Jr.

(1869–1932)

THEATRICAL IMPRESARIO

Kensico Cemetery
Valhalla, New York

The very name Ziegfeld conjures up visions of luscious femininity. Chorus girls were run-of-the-mill in anyone else's show, but Ziegfeld's finely tuned sense of style gave them an air of distinction and raised his shows above the merely splashy.

The "Glorifier of the American Girl" was hell-bent for perfection. To achieve his spectacular, fast-paced, never-never land, he oversaw every detail of his productions, including the most elegant set designs ever seen, and the graceful musical scores that he thought nothing of demanding from the likes of Jerome Kern or George Gershwin within three weeks' time. He carried little colored ribbons in his pocket, and on one occasion he changed the color scheme for an entire show, shortly before opening night, to match one of them.

In a frenetic attempt to resume his flamboyant pace after a bout with pneumonia, he imported flocks of show girls to his New York estate while his wife, Billie Burke, was working in California. The carousers scattered when, having heard his voice falter on a radio program, Billie returned to find the impresario pale and somehow shriveled in appearance, but eager to embark on a revival of *Show Boat*. But his doctors insisted that Ziegfeld slow down, and his wife took him back to California for a rest, hoping also to escape the creditors and process servers who hovered around him like gnats around a camper. On the train, he was bedded down with ice packs because of the heat and, often delirious, rambled on incoherently about his zigzagging past.

Once in California, he rallied sufficiently to send off six thousand dollars' worth of telegrams and to make eighty-dollar phone calls. Yet it was only a matter of days before he was in the hospital, where painful mustard treatments made him weep. He died in a room permeated by the scent of tuberoses, minutes before his wife could reach his bedside.

Ziegfeld never attended funerals, and his own was a simple service at the mortuary. His body was laid to rest in the mausoleum at Forest Lawn, that "final booking" for Hollywood's gaudy and famous. Forty-two years later the fabulous showman was taken across the continent and reinterred beside Billie Burke under a plain tablet near this statue—not of some Follies girl, but erected in memory of his mother-in-law.

Vernon Blyth Castle
(1887–1918)

Irene Foote Castle
(1893–1969)
DANCERS

*Woodlawn Cemetery
Bronx, New York*

Like Scott and Zelda Fitzgerald, Vernon and Irene Castle were the darlings of their era. Their heyday, however, was briefer, more innocent, and came a decade earlier. The Castles' syncopated elegance gave grace to the dance craze. They introduced the Hesitation Waltz, going up instead of down on the downbeat, the Castle Walk, and the Maxixe. Shopkeepers and cafe society alike imitated them, from Irene's bobbed hair and ease of dressing to their fox trot. Dancing schools spread the contagion.

The magic began in a Paris café in 1911 when, at the request of a headwaiter who had befriended the struggling couple, the Castles danced on the spur of the moment for visiting Russian royalty. The audience was enchanted, and that spark ignited a bright flame of success that skipped across the Atlantic and lasted until World War I. Then Vernon Castle—he dropped the Blyth early in his career—sailed to his native England to serve in the Royal Flying Corps. After two years of meritorious action over German territory, he returned to the United States to train American aviators at Fort Worth, Texas, where his aeronautical verve and style endeared him to his compatriots. Death came when he stalled his plane trying to avoid a midair collision. Tears streamed down the faces of his comrades as they recovered his twisted body from the wreckage.

Irene Castle never danced professionally again. She married three more times; her fourth husband, Charles Enzinger, died in 1959 and is buried beside her. Yet the monument, with its poignant figure sculpted by Sally Farnham, unites Vernon and Irene Castle once again in death. Late in life, Irene Castle, a fervent antivivisectionist, who had founded an animal shelter called Orphans of the Storm, stated, "Dancing was fun and I needed the money, but Orphans of the Storm comes from my heart. It's more important." Her will requested that "Humanitarian" be engraved, as it was, on her tombstone.

Ironically, the Castles' inscriptions say nothing about dancing.

MY BELOVED HVSBAND
VERNON CASTLE BLYTH
BORN MAY 2, 1887
WAS KILLED FEB. 15, 1918
IN THE SERVICE OF HIS COVNTRY
CROIX DE GVERRE

IRENE CASTLE
McLAVCHLIN ENZINGER
HVMANITARIAN
BORN APRIL 7, 1893
DIED JANVARY 25, 1969

Artists

Our painters, sculptors, and photographers portrayed the American style in a deeper, reflective sense.

Mathew B. Brady
(1823/4–1896)
PHOTOGRAPHER

Congressional Cemetery
Washington, D.C.

Mathew B. Brady (the middle initial stood for nothing) was the photographer laureate of the Civil War. Photography was a new medium, and the idea of taking it out of the studio and onto the battlefield was precocious. But Brady's recording of the war's pathetic horror was only a sideline. When he came to Lincoln and asked for permission "to go onto the battlefields with my cameras," he was already established as the leading portrait photographer in the country. It was as if Bachrach had presented himself to Lyndon B. Johnson and volunteered to photograph the Vietnam war at his own expense.

We have a special affection for Mathew Brady because, more than a century ago, he set about collecting the illustrious living with the same enthusiasm we hunt their graves. Brady made his reputation by enticing all manner of eminent citizens into his studio for sittings. At one time or another, virtually every contemporary American of any importance winced as Brady's "immobilizer" gripped their heads to keep them still for the long exposure. Their biographies are replete with examples of his work, and our perception of these forefathers is sharper because Brady gave us the opportunity to look them in the face. Among his subjects in these pages were Edwin Booth, John Brown, Horace Greeley, Samuel F. B. Morse (who taught Brady the early art of the daguerreotype), and Walt Whitman.

After the war, Brady never really regained his eminence as a portraitist. The government purchased two thousand of his wartime plates for twenty-five thousand dollars, a fraction of their admitted value, but after this was exhausted Brady lived in abject poverty. In his last year he was afflicted with kidney trouble, but absorbed himself in plans for an exhibition of his photographs at Carnegie Hall in New York. By December he became so weak that he was admitted to the "alms ward" at Presbyterian Hospital, where he spent his last Christmas and New Years. He died January 15, 1896, of chronic diffuse nephritis, two weeks before the exhibition was scheduled to open.

His exact year of birth is lost, although his death certificate gives his age as seventy-two, which gibes with his own statement that "I go back to near 1823–1824." But his year of death is certain, and it is unfortunate that whoever supplied the dates for his gravestone got both of them wrong.

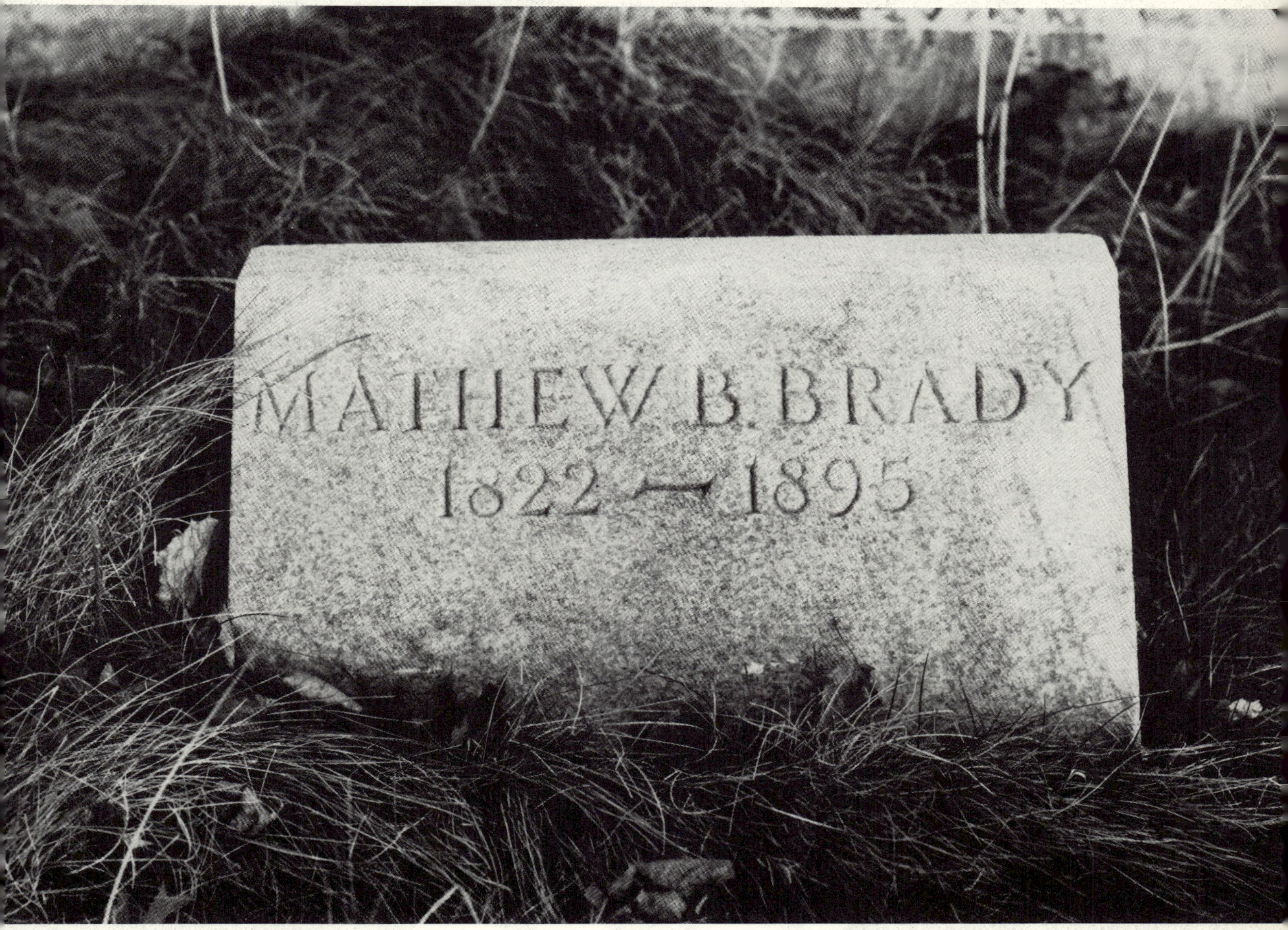
MATHEW B. BRADY
1822 — 1895

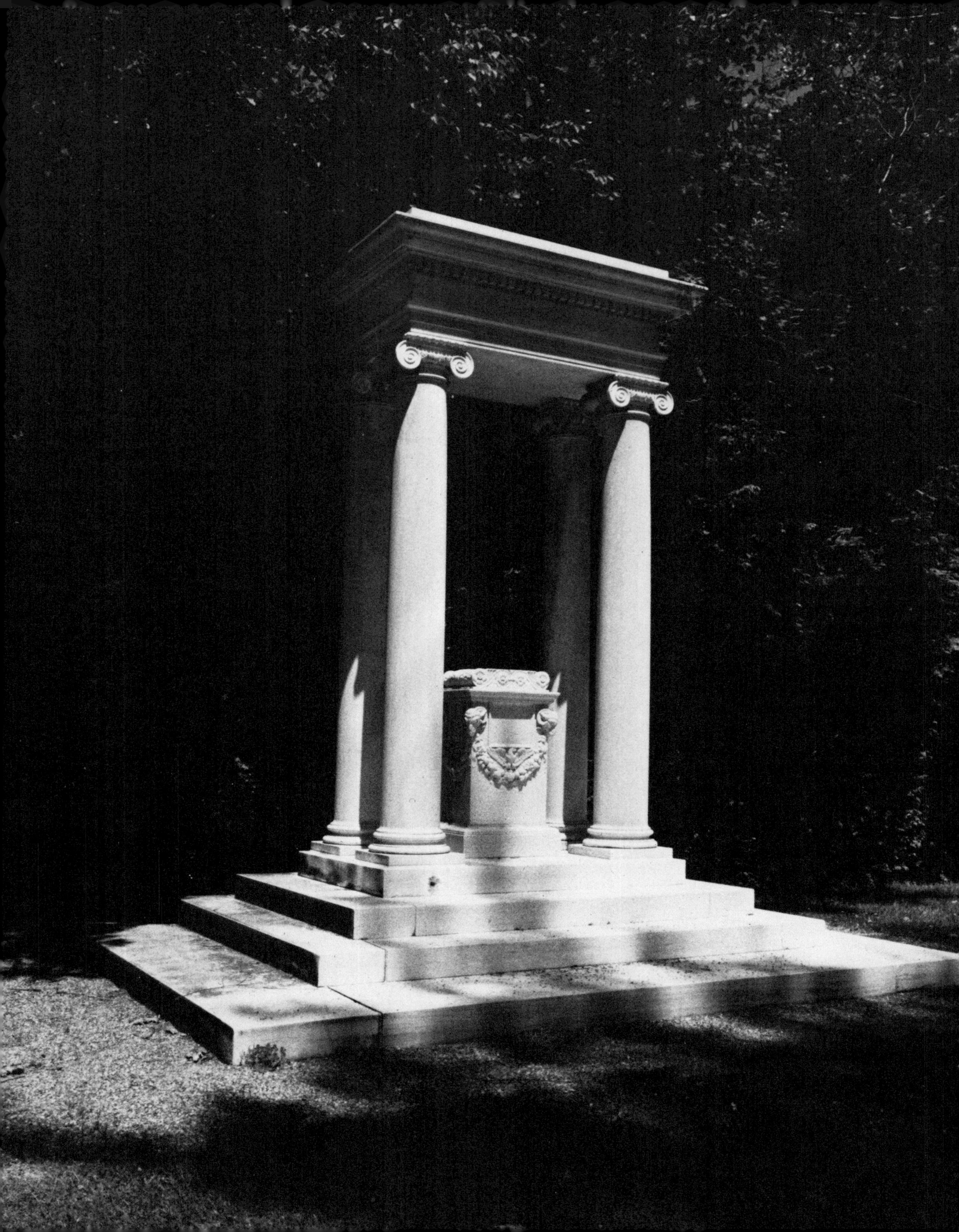

Augustus Saint-Gaudens
(1848–1907)
SCULPTOR

Aspet
Cornish, New Hampshire

Nannies shielded the eyes of their charges when the copper weather vane on top of the new Madison Square Garden was unveiled in 1891. But New York dandies pulled out field glasses and trained their sights on the naked Diana three-hundred feet above, poised on one foot to shoot her arrow toward the direction of the wind.

Ordinarily, the work of Augustus Saint-Gaudens did not create such a brouhaha. It was an era of genteel sculpture, of heroic bronze figures, their draperies flapping in a permanent breeze, striding toward the horizon of a shimmering, perfect world. Saint-Gaudens dominated American sculpture during this period. He began his prolific career as a cameo cutter, and he maintained a craftsmanlike approach through the years of bas-relief portraits and monumental commissions to the time not long before his death when he designed the last twenty-dollar gold piece.

There are charming Saint-Gaudens cherubs still to be found in cemeteries, where falling leaves tickle their frolicsome bodies; and the thoroughbred grace of his young mistress and model, Davida, materializes in a pink marble statue of an angel on a tomb in Newport, Rhode Island. Indeed, perhaps the sculptor's most famous statue is in a Washington, D.C., cemetery. It is the haunting bronze figure, with hand raised to covering veil, that Henry Adams commissioned as a memorial for his wife after her suicide. In preparation for its execution, Saint-Gaudens studied photographs and drawings of the oriental Buddha and later said that the figure, titleless but popularly known as "Grief," represented something "beyond pain, and beyond joy."

Saint-Gaudens did not design his own monument at Aspet, his New Hampshire home. Originally it was done in wood by an assistant as the setting for a masque held on the premises in 1905, not long after Saint-Gaudens had recuperated from one of several operations to remove a malignant intestinal tumor. The same assistant was with "the Saint," as his helpers referred to him, several days before he died. Sitting on a veranda and looking out at the setting sun, Saint-Gaudens remarked, "It's very beautiful here, but I want to go farther away."

After the Saint's death, his widow, Augusta, concentrated on the appropriate preservation of his memory. His home and studio became a sanctum and eventually a National Historic Site. Augusta had his ashes, originally buried in Windsor, Vermont, returned to Aspet and placed beneath the templelike monument, redone in Vermont marble.

Edward Hopper

(1882–1967)
PAINTER

Oak Hill Cemetery
Nyack, New York

Edward Hopper knew what he wanted and expressed it simply. "What I wanted to do was to paint sunlight on the side of a house." That is what he did, giving us a vision of the American scene stripped, despite an often-brilliant palette, to its essentials of light and shadow. When a friend compared his work to that of Mondrian, Hopper smiled and said, "You kill me." His aims were his own, and who can look at an ordinary clapboard house or an all-night coffee shop, with its light cutting into the surrounding darkness, without seeing them as Hopper leads us to see?

Hopper made his last trip to France in 1910. "The light was different from anything I had ever known," he wrote, but he knew that the luminosity of France was not for him. He returned to the steady, bolder light of his own country, where for the next half century he painted with a native directness.

His subjects were what was around him. His figures—an usherette in a dim movie house, a woman in a hotel room with a letter in her lap, a man by gas pumps across from pine woods—appear as part of his unmistakably American landscape, in which the effect is one of peculiar isolation, a sense of stillness, as if in the eye of a hurricane. Hopper did not talk much about the people he painted, or the hills, or ocean swells. To say "I liked those angles" sufficed.

As fads changed, Hopper did not. He continued to work, producing only a few paintings a year, in his own way; and recognition did not alter the simple patterns of his life. For over fifty years he lived on Washington Square in New York City. He and his wife, who also painted, often ate food from cans in their closet-size kitchen, tucked between two studios and a bedroom. Hopper died there, beneath the roof he had painted with the sun bursting on the angles of pipes and skylights, which cast shadows like those of the stones near his grave. The cemetery where he is buried overlooks the Tappan Zee, a wide expanse of the Hudson River, which, as a boy, he had sketched from the porch of his family's house.

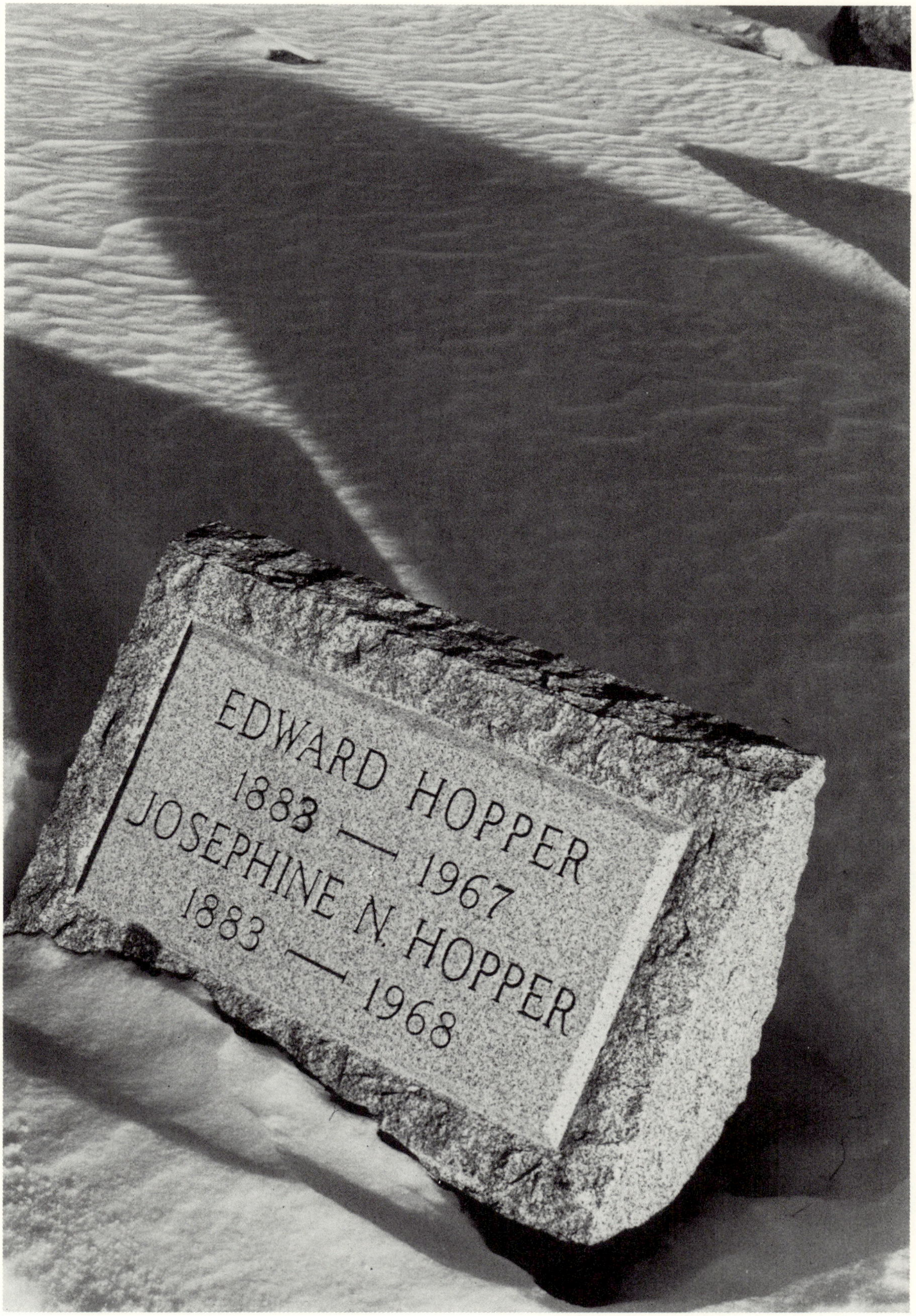
EDWARD HOPPER
1882 — 1967
JOSEPHINE N. HOPPER
1883 — 1968

Tunesmiths

We save for last the group we think lasts longest. As the composer said to the writer, "The audience doesn't leave the theater whistling your lyrics." We whistle these people into immortality.

John Philip Sousa

(1854–1932)
BANDMASTER/COMPOSER

Congressional Cemetery
Washington, D.C.

The sousaphone took his name, and the United States Marine Band, which he conducted for twelve years, came by its classy style from him. The name John Philip Sousa is synonymous with brightly orchestrated band music. Sousa composed over a hundred marches with titles like "The March Past of the Rifle Regiment," "The Beau Ideal March," and "The High School Cadets." Ideals? High school cadets? It was a different era. The Sousa Band, which he formed in 1892, was the smash hit of the concert circuit, and you can bet your belly button there were no drug problems in *that* outfit.

Sousa was a violin soloist at the age of eleven, and a boy enlistee at thirteen in the Marine Band, where his father played the trombone. He married and stayed married to a girl as pretty as a melody. Episcopalian in religion, Republican in politics, and patriotic by nature, Sousa toured in the United States and abroad by train and steamship. He never swore, paid well, and enjoyed the total loyalty of his snappily uniformed musicians, whom he conducted in an estimated thirty-thousand concerts.

One March evening, in 1932, Sousa finished conducting a rehearsal in Reading, Pennsylvania, and laid down his baton, one of the fifteen-cent variety, which he bought by the carton. It was his last rehearsal and "The Stars and Stripes Forever" was the final number. He had once said, "If you hear of Sousa retired, you'll hear of Sousa dead." His fifty-plus years as a bandmaster ended when he died the same night, after a heart attack in his hotel room. The next day the band followed his casket to the railroad station, playing in the rain. The March King had retired.

Sousa was buried with full military honors in Washington, D.C. George M. Cohan and Sigmund Romberg were honorary pallbearers. The only eulogy was music, and as white horses began pulling the caisson toward the cemetery, the Marine Band struck up his "Semper Fidelis" in dirge tempo.

The musical fragment carved on his gravestone is the familiar refrain from "The Stars and Stripes Forever," which we all learned as kids as "Be kind to your web-footed friends . . ."

SOUSA
— LEADER —
UNITED STATES MARINE BAND
1880 — 1892
JOHN PHILIP
SOUSA
MAR. 6, 1932

Sergei Vasilyevich Rachmaninoff

(1873–1943)

CONDUCTOR, PIANIST, COMPOSER

Kensico Cemetery
Valhalla, New York

Sergei Rachmaninoff, who had made his home in this country since the Bolshevik revolution, but became an American citizen less than two months before his death, was one of the towering figures of our contemporary music world. He began his career as a brilliant conductor in Russia and was one of the mightiest pianists of the twentieth century. But his brilliance in the ephemeral art of interpretation is eclipsed by the endearing and enduring quality of his compositions. Sometimes accused of excessive romanticism and dismissed as a Tchaikovskian sentimentalist, the fact remains that he wrote—unlike Charles Ives—music that people liked to hear. His famous Prelude in C-sharp Minor, which he tossed off as a boy, plagued him the rest of his life, as audiences clamored to hear it as an encore. And his Second Piano Concerto—composed after a period of intense depression and dedicated to his shrink—is surely the most popular work of its kind in the modern American repertoire.

His dour appearance, with closely cropped hair, bulldog scowl, and enormous ears, masked an intensely private and sensitive man. He adored children, farming, and driving, which he said gave him the same inner calm as conducting—"complete mastery of myself and of the forces, musical or mechanical, at my disposal." He was generous to a fare-thee-well, once donating the entire proceeds of a New York recital to Russian war relief. In his last years, he wondered whether he had spread his genius too thinly over the musical table. "I have hunted three hares," he reminisced, meaning conducting, performing, and composing. "Can I be sure that I have killed one of them?"

When he died in California of melanoma, a highly malignant form of cancer that overwhelmed him within a few weeks, the world agreed that he had killed all three of them. Bells tolled in the tower of the Russian Orthodox Church as the ageless requiem mass was chanted, the mourners standing in the chairless church according to custom. Another mass was sung in New York, and the Boston Symphony Orchestra, of which he had twice declined the post of conductor, played his "Isle of the Dead" at Carnegie Hall as a memorial. Originally destined to be returned to Russia, his body was entombed instead on the crest of a hill in suburban New York beneath a strikingly simple granite monument in the shape of the Russian cross.

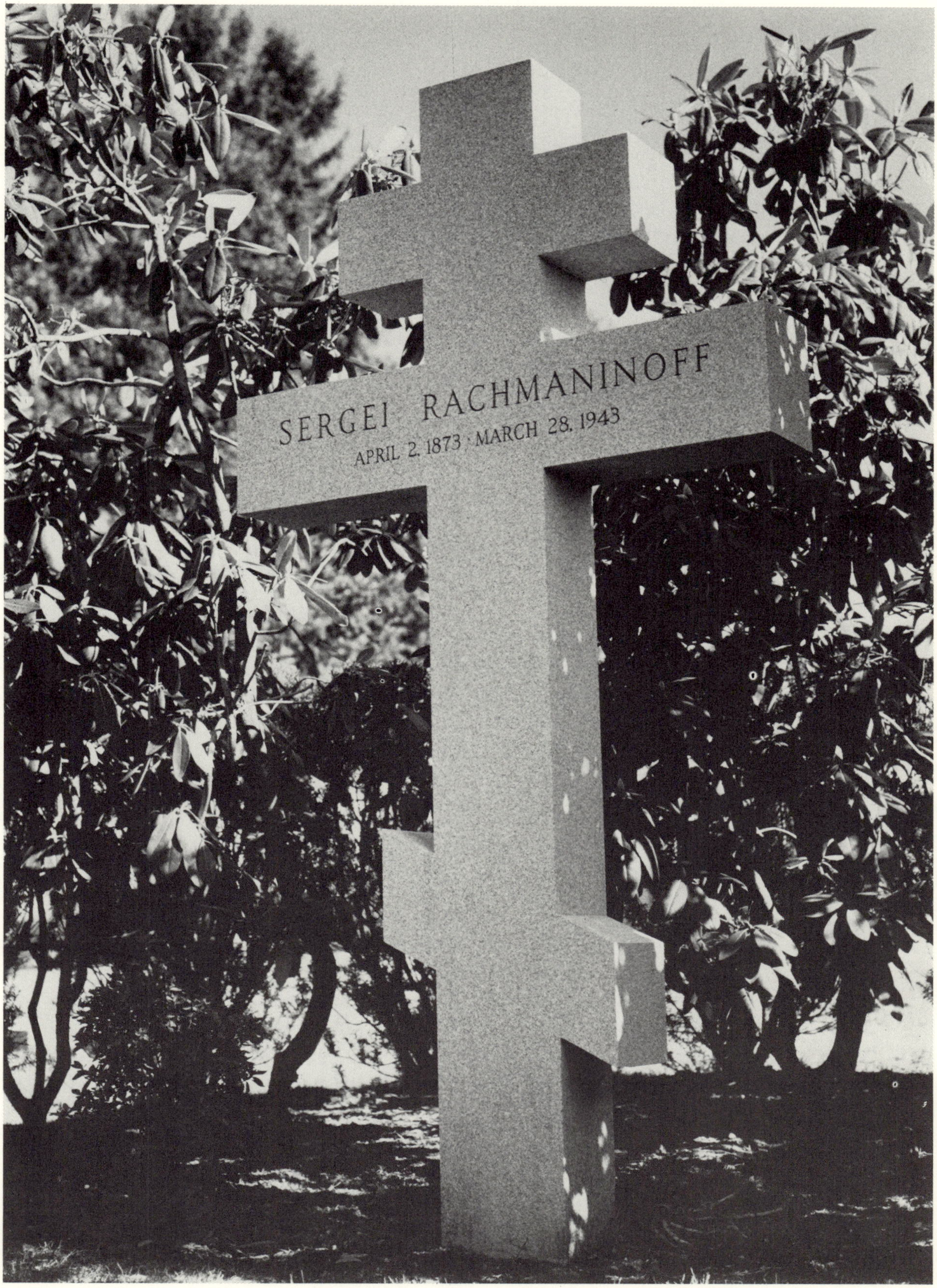
SERGEI RACHMANINOFF
APRIL 2. 1873 · MARCH 28. 1943

Charles Edward Ives

(1874–1954)
COMPOSER

Wooster Cemetery
Danbury, Connecticut

People didn't whistle the music of Charles Ives as they left the concert hall. Why wouldn't he give the people something they liked to hear? "I can't," said Ives. "I hear something different."

His sense of musical independence began under the tutelage of his father, a bandmaster and an unusual teacher, who had his students sing "Swanee River" in E-flat to an accompaniment in C-flat, in order, recalled Ives, "to stretch our ears." By the time he was a student at Yale, where his composition professor asked him if he had to "hog all those keys," Ives started "trying things on the side."

He continued to compose the way he wanted, "on the side" of the mainstream of the musical world. "Please don't try to make things nice," he once admonished his copyist. "All the wrong notes are *right*." Simultaneously, he shared a partnership in one of the country's most successful insurance brokerages, which enabled him to publish some of his compositions at his own expense.

What was it about his music that buffaloed copyists, baffled listeners, and bewildered performers because it was so difficult to play? It was music that recreated distinctly American impressions. One musical evocation is his picture of *The Fourth of July*, in which the holiday materializes in sound: familiar Yankee tunes, heavy hymns, the sounds of a town's brass band, and all the Independence Day hullabaloo, have their part in a dazzling symphonic display, with rhythms and harmonies run amuck. His work was called eccentric, and it took Schönberg and Stravinsky using, like Ives ten or fifteen years before them, the techniques of atonality, polyrhythms and polyharmonies, to make the public "stretch its ears."

Charles Ives received his first major award, the Pulitzer Prize, for his Third Symphony thirty-six years after its completion. After that, his music was more frequently performed, but he was seldom satisfied with the conducting. As he grew older, still restless, despising his infirmities, his musical audacity did not diminish. Perhaps one day his *Universe* Symphony will be performed as he envisioned it, with at least two full orchestras playing on mountaintops across a valley from each other.

With his creative independence intact, Ives died in New York City of complications following an operation. He is buried in the family plot on a Connecticut hillside, beside his wife, named Harmony.

CHARLES EDWARD IVES
OCTOBER 20, 1874
MAY 19, 1954
AND HIS WIFE
HARMONY TWICHELL
JUNE 4, 1876
APR. 4, 1969
AWAKE PSALTERY AND HARP: I MYSELF
WILL AWAKE RIGHT EARLY
Ps. 108:2

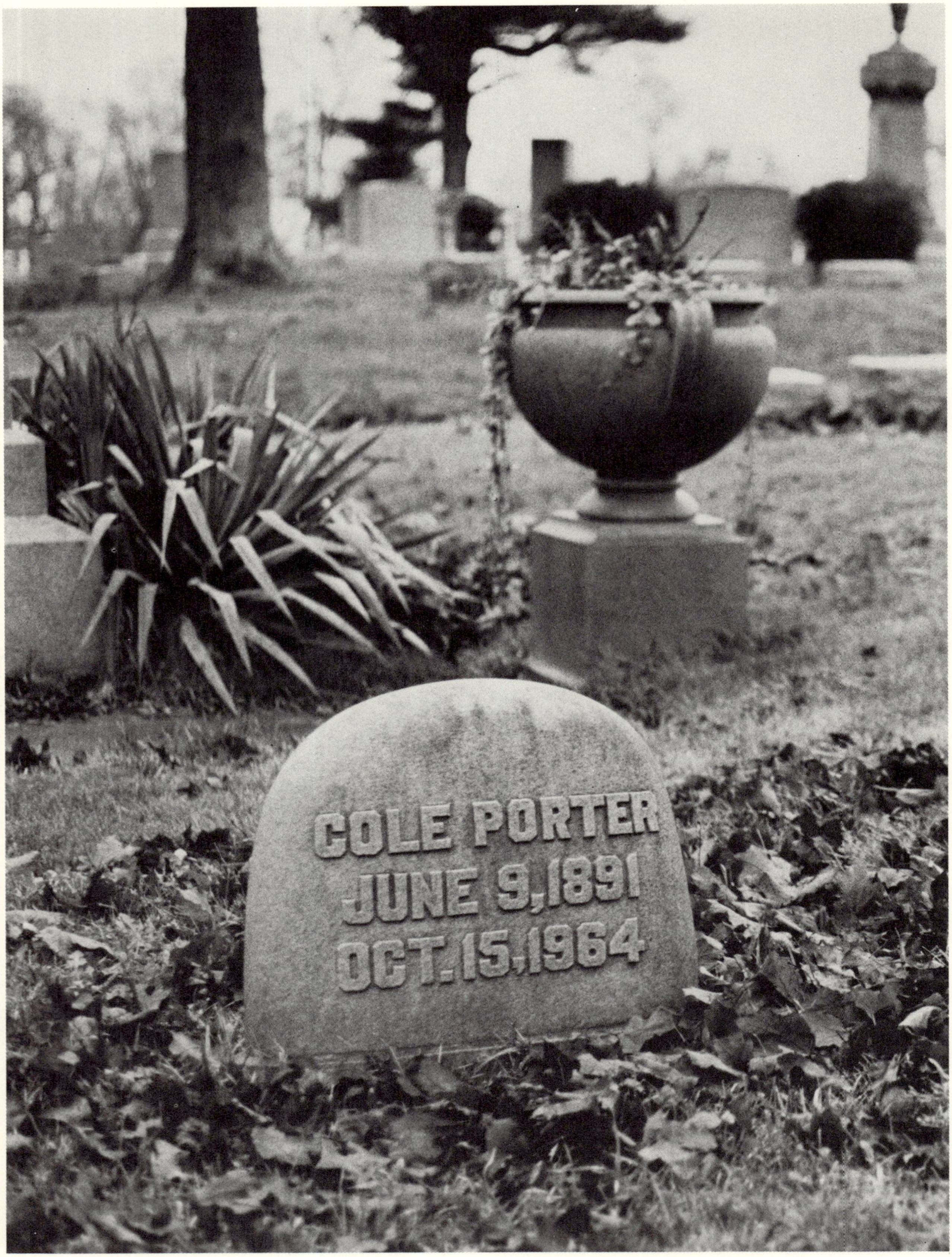
COLE PORTER
JUNE 9, 1891
OCT. 15, 1964

Cole Albert Porter

(1891–1964)

COMPOSER, LYRICIST

Mount Hope Cemetery
Peru, Indiana

Part of the magnetism of New York is that it attracts the choicest iron from elsewhere, and it is always ironic to hear that a successful and prominent New Yorker was raised on a farm. One can hardly think of a New Yorker who better epitomized the gaiety and sophistication of the city than Cole Porter, who grew up in Peru (Pee-roo), Indiana, literally on the banks of the Wabash, and went from writing Hoosier songs to such immortals as "Begin the Beguine," "Night and Day," and "I Get a Kick Out of You."

Cole Porter spent most of his adult life in New York, and the cosmopolitan wit that so characterizes his songs completely overshadows the haunting thread of sadness that permeates so many of them. Perhaps this sadness reflects his years of suffering as a result of a riding accident on Long Island in 1937, which crushed his legs and crippled him for life. Or perhaps it was homesickness; because when he finally succumbed to the ordeal of twenty-seven years of physical agony and some thirty-five operations, including the amputation of his right leg, and his last will and testament was opened and read, it began this way:

FIRST:

I DIRECT my Executors to arrange for my burial in Peru, Indiana. I FURTHER DIRECT my Executors to arrange for no funeral or memorial service, but only for a private burial service to be conducted by the Pastor of the First Baptist Church of Peru, in the presence of my relatives and dear friends. At such service I request said Pastor to read the following quotation from the Bible:

> I am the resurrection, and the life:
> he that believeth in me, though he were
> dead, yet shall he live: And whosoever
> liveth and believeth in me shall never die.

and to follow such quotation with The Lord's Prayer.

I request that the foregoing be substantially the entire burial service, and that neither said Pastor nor anyone else deliver any memorial address whatsoever. I particularly direct that there be no service of any kind for me in New York City.

And so, in a last supreme gesture of defiance to the city that made him what he was, Cole Porter went back to a modest grave on a small hill in the black Indiana soil of the little town that had brought him forth.

George Gershwin
(1898–1937)
COMPOSER

Westchester Hills Cemetery
Hastings-on-Hudson, New York

In February 1937, when he was at the height of his career and not yet forty, George Gershwin blacked out for a few seconds while performing his *Concerto in F* with the Los Angeles Philharmonic and had a sensation of smelling burning rubber. A checkup revealing nothing amiss, Gershwin continued swinging in the giddy orbit that had made him America's musical idol and Hollywood's leading ladies' man. In his spare time, Gershwin worked furiously on the scores for *A Damsel in Distress*, starring Fred Astaire, and *The Goldwyn Follies*, two of the songs from which—"Love Walked In" and "Love is Here to Stay," the last song he ever wrote—became among his greatest hits posthumously.

But Gershwin was becoming weaker all the time. By June, he began to develop headaches and dizzy spells, always accompanied by the sickening burning smell, and loss of coordination. He became listless and irritable and light bothered him. Once again he entered the hospital but refused permission for a painful spinal tap, which might have demonstrated the cause of his illness.

On July 9, Gershwin fell into a deep coma. Unconscious, the test he had wakingly refused revealed the presence of a fulminating brain tumor. Through the intervention of the White House, a noted Eastern brain surgeon was plucked off a yacht in Chesapeake Bay by the Coast Guard and flown to Newark, where another plane stood by to rush him to California. Gershwin's doctors decided to operate without him, but it was already too late. A few hours after the operation, "the singer of the songs of America's soul," "the man who said he had more tunes in his head than he could put down on paper in a hundred years," died without regaining consciousness.

Forty years later, with his tunes in our ears every day, it is impossible to accept that George Gershwin is dead. Pianist Oscar Levant recalls an overnight Pullman ride, when George pre-empted the lower berth, leaving Oscar to shinny into the upper. "Upper berth—lower berth," pronounced George. "That's the difference between talent and genius." Gershwin was thirty-eight years old when he died, scarcely older than Mozart. We ponder how much more each might have left us had he been permitted to live, and we are left with a sense of the awful finality of death and, at the same time, a sense of joy for the gift of life, however short.

GERSHWIN